What Successful Principals Do!

169 Tips for Principals

Franzy Fleck

EYE ON EDUCATION

EYE ON EDUCATION
6 DEPOT WAY WEST, SUITE 106
LARCHMONT, NY 10538
(914) 833–0551
(914) 833–0761 fax
www.eyeoneducation.com

Library of Congress Cataloging-in-Publication Data

Fleck, Franzy.
   What successful principals do! : 169 tips for principals / Franzy Fleck.
       p. cm.
     Includes bibliographical references and index.
     ISBN 1-930556-97-7
   1. School principals—Handbooks, manuals, etc. 2. School management
and organization. I. Title.
     LB2831.9.F54 2005
     371.2'012—dc22

                                                    2004030214

109876543

Editorial and production services provided by
Richard H. Adin Freelance Editorial Services
52 Oakwood Blvd., Poughkeepsie, NY 12603-4112
(845-471-3566)

Also Available from EYE ON EDUCATION

What Great Principals Do *Differently*:
15 Things That Matter Most
Todd Whitaker

Great Quotes for Great Educators
Todd Whitaker and Dale Lumpa

What Great Teachers Do *Differently*:
14 Things That Matter Most
Todd Whitaker

BRAVO Principal!
Sandra Harris

Stepping Outside Your Comfort Zone:
Lessons for School Leaders
Nelson Beaudoin

Dealing with Difficult Teachers, Second Edition
Todd Whitaker

Dealing with Difficult Parents
(And with Parents in Difficult Situations)
Todd Whitaker and Douglas Fiore

Motivating & Inspiring Teachers
The Educational Leader's Guide for Building Staff Morale
Todd Whitaker, Beth Whitaker, and Dale Lumpa

The Principal as Instructional Leader:
A Handbook for Supervisors
Sally J. Zepeda

Instructional Leadership for School Improvement
Sally J. Zepeda

Supervision Across the Content Areas
Sally J. Zepeda and R. Stewart Mayers

The ISLLC Standards in Action:
A Principal's Handbook
Carol Engler

Harnessing the Power of Resistance:
A Guide for Educators
Jared Scherz

Standards of Practice for Teachers:
A Brief Handbook
P. Diane Frey, Mary Jane Smart, and Sue A. Walker

Achievement Now!
How To Assure No Child is Left Behind
Dr. Donald J. Fielder

Teaching Matters:
Motivating & Inspiring Yourself
Todd and Beth Whitaker

101 Answers for New Teachers and Their Mentors:
Effective Teaching Tips for Daily Classroom Use
Annette L. Breaux

Data Analysis for Continuous School Improvement
Victoria L. Bernhardt

School Leader Internship: Developing, Monitoring,
and Evaluating Your Leadership Experience
Gary Martin, William Wright, and Arnold Danzig

Handbook on Teacher Evaluation:
Assessing and Improving Performance
James Stronge & Pamela Tucker

Handbook on Educational Specialist Evaluation:
Assessing & Improving Performance
James Stronge & Pamela Tucker

Handbook on Teacher Portfolios
for Evaluation and Professional Development
Pamela Tucker & James Stronge

Dedication

I would like to thank my parents, Louis and Helen Fleck, and my parents-in-law, Larry and Phyllis Brown. Their support, energy, and confidence have always inspired me to do my best.

Many thanks to my children, Tyler Farron and Gentry Elizabeth, for being the best cheerleaders of anything I do. Ty: my son, my sunshine, my pride and joy, my outdoorsman, your love for nature and the simple pleasures help to remind me to live each day to the fullest. Your wit, charm, and positive energy make our home come alive. It's never the same when you are gone. Thank you for your support, for making us laugh, and for your practical wisdom that makes you special. I thank you for being my sidekick when I am with my friends and allowing me to hang out with you and your friends. I thank you for being a *real* man, protecting the weak and needy, willing to stop those who are wrong, being a good sport, and being your sister and mother's protector.

Gentry: my daughter, my shining star, your love and kindness make our home warm and glow. I thank God for bringing you into our lives. Your unconditional love and support remind us that family is the most important thing in the world. You are wise beyond your years and are always putting others first. I thank you for making us think, and for your belief in us, your gentle way, your high value system of fairness, and your poetic words of inspiration.

Finally, I can never, ever give enough thanks to my wife, and best friend, Kristy Fleck. Your continual love and support has made me a better person than I could be without you. Since our marriage, you have inspired me and supported my efforts with your positive outlook on life. You have inspired me by saying, "Things have a way of working out. If it was meant to be, then it will be. God has a plan for us." And my favorite, "Lord, I hope I do something tomorrow that makes you proud of me." All that I am and hope to be, I owe to you and am truly blessed to be a part of your life.

Acknowledgments

My sincere appreciation is extended to Dr. Todd Whitaker, my mentor and committee chairperson, for his continual vision, support, enthusiasm, and friendship. You are the best. You are always willing to give of yourself; your practical wisdom is unmatched.

Dr. Greg Ulm and Dr. Beth Whitaker, I express my gratitude for your words of encouragement, insightful comments, and caring attitude. I would like to thank Superintendents Phillip Schoffstall and Sandra Nixon, and Principal Jack Woods, who served as my early mentors and modeled exemplary leadership.

To Dr. Phillip Schlechty, George Thompson, Tom Johnson, and the staff at the Schlechty Center for Leadership in School Reform, your words of wisdom and actions were inspiring. You're always making me think. Many thanks to Dr. Charles Harrington, Dr. John Gray, Carl Riddle, Dr. Robert Boyd, Glen Howell, Ken Wempe, Nancy Woods, Rebecca Heil, Judith Barnes, Terri Alvey, Kristy Dedmond, and Gene Teriac; each of you has assisted me in some way.

To the teachers and staff at Princeton Middle School and Harper Elementary School, I am grateful for your patience and fairness, and for taking the time to teach me how to be a principal.

To Principals James Mason, Dan Gilbert, Steve Hauger, and James Issacs and the teachers, staff, and principals of the Evansville-Vanderburgh School Corporation : This book is more about you then for you. I thank the Bosse Attendance District Principals Lana Burton, Vicki Duncan, Patricia Edwards, Sheila Huff, Rance Ossenberg, and Robert Adams for their diligence, persistence, and vision to see what may be.

Many thanks to Libby Turner, Andy Chandler, Yvonne Knies, and Phil Wolter for their friendship, support, and willingness to give of their self in helping others. I would like to thank the many members of the Turoni's softball team. The players come and go, but the support, laughs, and stories get better with age.

To the teachers and principals from my early school days at Glenwood Elementary School and Benjamin Bosse High School: Your patience and guidance placed me on the right path. Your actions exemplified teamwork, family, and building positive relationships. To my professors at the University of Evansville and Indiana State University, your lessons and advice instilled in me the knowledge that I could make my dreams come true.

To my brothers and sisters Gwen, Louis, Emil, and Sharon, and brother- and sister-in-law Norman and Amy Browning, as well as other family members, I thank you for your belief in me.

I would also like to thank my publisher, Robert Sickles. His guidance and vision have enabled me to combine theory, leadership, and practical sense into one for my fellow educators.

Table of Contents

About the Author

Dr. Franzy Fleck is a principal and an associate professor in Evansville, Indiana. Dr. Fleck was a junior high teacher, middle school principal, and district administrator prior to coming to Evansville. He has been in education working with students at the elementary, middle school, high school, and university level.

Dr. Fleck has been published in the area of leadership effectiveness, motivation, administration, and leadership. In 2003, he was recognized for excellence in research and leadership by Indiana State University. Most recently, Dr. Fleck was involved in planning and developing the Educational Leadership and Administration program at the University of Southern Indiana where he serves as an associate professor.

Dr. Fleck is married to Kristy Fleck, an elementary teacher in Evansville. They have two children, Tyler and Gentry.

Preface

My interest in writing this book is a result of several experiences. First, I was blessed to have been a student in educational leadership, and I served on university leadership committees at Indiana State University. My ISU professors instilled a passion in me to use my leadership talents to serve others. Teaching is a rewarding profession. As a teacher, I was able to work with hundreds of students each day. My scope of influence as a teacher was limited to a certain number of students, however. School leadership enabled me to have a greater impact on children. Being a school leader meant that I could widen my base of influence and touch the lives of every student, teacher, parent, district administrator, and school community member; as a teacher, it was with a smaller set of individuals.

My second experience came as an assistant principal, district administrator, and then principal. I noticed that even though I felt prepared in the theoretical sense, I was not completely prepared in the practical sense. The university had prepared me well in theory to serve as a school leader, but practical knowledge was based on my teaching experiences and principal internship. A school leader must be prepared in theory and practical application. A marriage between theory and practical knowledge must coexist.

As a first year assistant principal in North Gibson School Corporation, I was blessed to have a wise principal and superintendent. It made me think about beginning administrators who enter a school as the only principal. Serving as an assistant principal allowed me the opportunity to learn and grow as a school leader. My experiences caused to me think about assistant principals who have poor principals as their only source of practical experience. What about beginning principals who have poor, weak, or unethical superintendents? What about beginning principals whose only sources of contact are poor principals in their school district, or superiors with limited experience as a principal or, even worse, no experience as a principal?

Many experienced principals and superintendents are too busy to help nurture beginning principals. They may have only limited knowledge and therefore are unable to help beginning principals with practical advice on running a successful school. Many superintendents and school board members are political creatures and sometimes offer advice accordingly. A good school decision and a good political school decision can be different. The demands of a principal are high, and many are forced to struggle through their beginning years. The life of a principal should not be a lonely and frustrating profession. This book's purpose is to give beginning principals a source of strategies that successful principals can use every day.

Third, a common concern among beginning principals is a lack of support and a sense of frustration during their first years. The demands of the school community can be overwhelming at times. Many eager and enthusiastic principals have earned their principal license with the dream of making a difference only to be smacked in the face with the reality of challenging students, unrealistic parents, poor teachers, weak superintendents, and demanding school communities. Why should beginning principals only learn through trial and error? A better approach must be used with those entering the principal field.

Fourth, I conceived the idea for writing this book based on my experiences developing and preparing aspiring principals. I was part of a group that helped the University of Southern Indiana develop a Principal License program. As an associate professor, I began writing short lessons that aspiring principals could use as a school leader, with the intent to marry theory and practical knowledge into one. My university work is to help prepare aspiring administrators with practical tips and strategies that will make their beginning years go smoother.

Beginning principals can be prepared with university theory, teaching experiences and their principal internship, but it can be better. This book's intent is to prepare a list of principal tips for beginning principals but also suggest strategies that veteran principals can use in their schools. The principalship can be both frustrating and rewarding. Many principals are returning to the classroom, taking early retirement, or leaving the field of education as a result of the frustrating aspects of the principal's role. Teachers need great principals. Students need great principals. Parents need great principals. In short, schools need great principals. If a beginning or veteran principal struggles, then there is little hope for beginning teachers to succeed. If teachers struggle, then there is little hope for students to succeed; if students struggle, then there is little hope for the future of our students, schools, and communities.

The final reason for writing this book is to help teachers be successful with their students and parents. The teaching profession, like the principal profession, can be as challenging as it is rewarding. Principals have to be on top of their game to help beginning and veteran teachers. Each year, more and more outstanding teachers are leaving the teaching profession. It is unacceptable for some of our best minds to leave the teaching profession. A key element to having successful students is to keep successful teachers in our schools. A key element to keeping successful teachers in our schools is to have successful principals in our schools. This book is designed to give successful tips that beginning and veteran principals should be using in their schools. This book is designed to give insight to help principals be successful and keep successful teachers in the field of education.

1

Beginning
the School Year

Build
Positive Relationships

Constant kindness can accomplish much. As the sun makes the ice melt, kindness causes misunderstanding, mistrust, and hostility to evaporate.

—Albert Schweitzer

Am I not destroying my enemies when I make friends of them?

—Abraham Lincoln

Leaders must take time to build positive relationships with all groups. Develop meaningful relationships with student groups, the student council, the national honor society, girls' athletic teams, boys' athletic teams, academic teams, music groups, and clubs, considering gender, religion, and race among the groups. Parents and their respective groups must be considered, too, as should businesses and community groups. A leader should consider exploring the yellow pages, local newspapers, and magazines to learn about groups in the community. The leader needs to have the pulse of each of these groups. Face-to-face contact with people is still the best way. Becoming interested in the students is an outstanding way to building positive relationships with the parents. Students will share your positive interactions with their parents and families. Working alongside, socializing with, and cheering on student groups, and meeting with people takes an enormous amount of time, but it's the best way to get to know people. A leader has to be constantly reaching out to others.

Communicate
Your Vision

Men often oppose a thing merely because they have had no agency in planning it, or because it may have been planned by those whom they dislike.

—Alexander Hamilton

Some people dream of worthy accomplishments, while others stay awake and do them.

—Anonymous

Make sure every employee understands your vision and philosophies. A leader needs to create a school vision centered on the needs of students, parents, teachers, businesses, and the community. Blanchard and Bowles (1993), in *Raving Fans,* say the secret to creating a vision is to decide what you want followed by discovering what the customer wants. It takes time to communicate a clear and concise vision with each employee. Teaching and communicating your philosophies is time well spent. Your employees will start to emulate your actions, which is a desired goal for a leader. Have frequent informal and formal conversations with staff throughout the year. Don't assume that employees understand your vision. Learn to visit, revisit, discuss, and reflect. A leader must ensure that employee actions are consistent with your vision and philosophies.

Unite Employees with a Mission Statement

If I have someone who believes in me, I can move mountains.

—Diana Ross

Imagination is the beginning of creation. You imagine what you desire, you will what you imagine and at last you create what you will.

—George Bernard Shaw

David Cottrell (2002), in Monday Morning Leadership, says that leaders should "keep the Main thing the Main thing." A leader has to be able to unite employees with an organizational mission. A mission statement tells all what the school is about. It should be clear, concise, and focused. A common mistake is to have a mission statement that is broad and general. There should be no misunderstanding as to the mission of the school. Keep it specific and limited. A leader should meet with employees to discuss and make sure every employee understands the corporate mission. Cottrell points out that employees commonly misinterpret the organization's mission. Don't assume that employees know the mission of the school. Ask your employees if they know what the main mission is. Engage in activities to thoroughly discuss the mission of the school and district. The leader has to ensure that all employees' activities are working in tandem with the school's mission. What if there is confusion on the school's mission? This confusion could have persons working against each other. Be sure to revisit your school mission each year.

Share Work Expectations with Staff

Pleasure in the job puts perfection in the work.

—Aristotle

Most school leaders start the year with a faculty meeting. This meeting is a time to see old friends, meet new friends, pass out papers or forms, motivate the staff, and discuss work expectations. An important discussion item is sharing work expectations with staff. The leader commonly shares personal philosophies such as being on time, modeling for students, and how to treat students. Common mistakes are to share expectations once at a faculty meeting assuming employees know and understand your expectations. Leaders should have frequent informal and formal conversations with the staff during the school year. The school leader should not assume that employees know expectations. Frequent conversations should help employees understand. Sometimes it takes several conversations to clearly communicate expectations. A second mistake is for a leader to address the entire staff for one person's misunderstanding. Don't send memos or e-mail the entire staff if only one or two individuals need reminders. A leader should address concerns privately with the individual. These frequent conversations should help employees understand your position and expectations.

Turn Cell Phones Off

Rudeness is the weak man's imitation of strength.

—Eric Hoffer

Create an environment where cell phones are turned off during the workday as well as during meetings and presentations. It's rude to have a cell phone ring during a presentation or meeting. My cell phone is turned off unless I'm in my car or alone. There is no excuse for a teacher to have a cell phone on during class time. Teachers are expected to be working with children. If the children are working independently, then the teacher should be giving individual attention to the students. Even a quick one-minute phone call is unacceptable. Cell phones that ring during a meeting, presentation, or class time send a message that the phone call is more important than the people in your meeting, the speaker, or your students.

Some leaders will argue that they have a crisis to address and are expecting a phone call. Leaders should teach their employees to become leaders. If a leader has to be called to address every crisis, he or she is becoming a crisis manager. Teach your employees to make decisions that fall within your philosophy and vision. Make it a policy to hire great employees, share visions and philosophies, give confidence, and expect them to make good decisions. If you, the principal, have to make every decision, then you don't need some of your employees because you are doing their work. Employees will surprise you with great results if you teach and give them confidence. They won't be perfect, but no one is. If you're going to be away, give instructions or guidelines to your staff, especially if you are dealing with a critical concern. Staff will learn how you would respond and will deal with the situation if you are unavailable. The first thing to address on returning to the building is to be updated on any concerns. Second, reassure staff decisions during your absence. Most people will know if they made an erroneous decision and will bring it up to you. This creates the opportunity to discuss and teach employees. We have to remember that we are investing in our employees and they will make mistakes. Occasionally you will have a major crisis that will demand your attention, but these situations are not that common.

Set Short-Term Goals to Motivate Employees

Method is much, technique is much, but inspiration is even more.

—Benjamin Cardozo

You can't wait for inspiration. You have to go after it with a club.

—Jack London

Leaders need to consider employees values when making decisions. Each person has a different set of values. What's important is different for each person. Reflect on each employee's value system before setting a goal. Set goals that respond to each person's own set of values. It will ensure the success rate.

Learn to set short-term goals that your employees can focus on with enthusiasm. It's easier to stay focused on a short-term goal. For example, most schools will set long-term improvement goals based on a state test. Although setting an improvement goal on a high stakes test is important, schools need to set short-term goals that are a part of the long-term goal. It is common to develop and plan a long-term goal but forget short-term goals that build on each other and lead up to a long-term goal. In this same example, learn to set short-term goals that focus on the state standards. Encourage teachers to set shorter goals than a nine- or six-week grading report. Set weekly or biweekly goals that focus on state standards achieved in each classroom for each student. A short and simple three-question test that addresses a state standard could be provided to each student. Setting short-term weekly goals will also improve student achievement on annual high-stakes testing. Finally, be sure to celebrate short-term goal successes. People will usually have more inspiration working on short-term goals. Motivation and inspiration will decrease as the time length of the goal increases.

Encourage Staff to Set Improvement Goals

Obstacles are those frightful things you see when you take your eyes off your goal.

Henry Ford

Success seems to be largely a matter of hanging on after others have let go.

—William Feather

Schools are supposed to help students grow academically and prepare for the future. Teachers are supposed to take each student from their current learning ability and improve on that level. Staff should be expected to grow as well. Principals have to help teachers set improvement goals while encouraging pursuit of professional development opportunities. Encourage staff to submit two to three written goals each year. Goals should be measurable and focus on student achievement, school improvement, and professional development. Goals could be based on the individual, grade, department, or team. Frequently discuss progress on these goals during the school year with the employees. Finally, have an end-of-the-year conference with each employee to discuss goal successes, goal setbacks, and goal plans for the upcoming year. Research conducted found significant differences with principals who encouraged setting yearly improvement goals, talked about teacher progress, and regularly tried to help improve their teachers. Principals spent more time with less effective teachers on these issues than with their more effective teachers (Fleck, 2003). This is supported by research that effective principals apparently recognize the unique styles of and needs of teachers and help teachers achieve their own performance goals (Bossert, Dwyer, Rowan, & Lee, 1982). It is interesting that principals talked with less effective teachers on setting yearly improvement goals but encouraged their more effective teachers to pursue professional development opportunities and to stay current on educational issues. Ubben and Hughes (1997) shared Deming's research findings that skill improvement should be required for all members of the school, and a vigorous program of education and self improvement should be instituted.

Make Goals Measurable

What gets measured gets done.

—Tom Peters

The indispensable first step to getting the things you want out of life is this: Decide what you want.

—Ben Stein

Leaders learn to set measurable goals. The principal should establish short-term goals, intermediate goals, and long-term goals that can be measured. A common goal is to pass an academic assessment test administered by the state. The leader should be setting short-term goals leading up to the state test. Don't let one state test determine your school's success. Set short-term academic goals weekly or monthly. Give short three- to four-question assessments to see if students are achieving results. Be results-oriented and make all goals measurable. Ask yourself, "How will I assess or measure this goal? What data will be used and collected? How will I know if I succeeded?"

Set the Tone
for Others to Follow

For a manager to be perceived as a positive manager, they need a four to one positive to negative contact ratio.

—Kenneth Blanchard

Never do anything you wouldn't be willing to explain on television.

—Arjay Miller

The leader sets the tone. It is important for the leader to be a positive role model. You will be amazed, how often others are watching the leader's behaviors. The building will take on the personality of the leader. A leader has to be aware of their actions. School leaders need to set a good example for our students and community. Employees look to you and will model your attitudes and behaviors. Every day provides an opportunity for school personnel to teach others how to behave through their words and actions. It may be more critical for children who lack positive role models in their lives. A leader needs to be aware of any negative action or comment. Any inappropriate comment will be shared with others. Don't say anything that you wouldn't be able to explain in the newspaper or on television. Be positive. Act positive. Be visible. Make positive phone calls. Build positive relationships. Interact with students, parents, and the community. Be a lifelong learner. Read. Be involved. Enjoy each day.

Be on Time

Time is the coin of your life. It is the only coin you have, and only you can determine how it will be spent. Be careful lest you let other people spend it for you.

—Carl Sandburg

Encourage staff to start every period, meeting, and program on time. Leaders need to model and encourage timeliness. Start meetings on time. Teach and expect your employees to be on time. Don't create a crisis because of poor planning. A copy machine malfunction is not a good excuse. Great teachers plan ahead and will have materials ready a few days prior to the lesson. Poor weather means you have to leave earlier than normal. Don't get in the habit of allowing excuses for lateness. Train yourself and staff to excuse yourself if you are in a meeting. People will understand if you have a scheduled responsibility. Instruct your staff to start class on time. Teachers should be in the habit of standing at the door during passing periods. Being at the door when students are dismissed and entering the class will help students move quickly during passing periods. This not only helps to eliminate potential problems and build relationships with students, but it will help class start sooner. These small minutes will add up as the year progresses. For example, saving 2 minutes each period will add up to 12 minutes during the school day for a student enrolled in six classes; 12 minutes will add up to 60 minutes during a week; saving 60 minutes a week will total to more than five school days during the course of a year. At the elementary level, teachers need to be reminded to pick classes up on time or early but never be late; a teacher's day often relies on others with time issues. For example, Mrs. Gibson may not be able to start her assigned planning period until Mrs. Cobb arrives to start class. Another teacher being a few minutes late is major if a lunch period is only 40 minutes. Keep in mind that teachers end up with less than 40 minutes for lunch if they tidy up the room, pick up messages in the office, take a bathroom break, walk to lunch, and arrive early to start their next lesson. With this in mind, a few minutes is a big deal. Create an environment where you are working on "Lombardi Time," where if you arrive 10 minutes early, then you are considered on time.

Dress Professionally Every Day

In a tuxedo, I'm a star. In regular clothes, I'm nobody.

—Dean Martin

If you have a question about how appropriately to dress, then err on the conservative side. Teachers, secretaries, custodians, students, and parents will follow the principal's lead on how to dress at school. Each level will usually dress equal or down a level from the boss. Teachers will dress equal or down a level from the principal. Students will dress equal or, more likely, down a level or two from the teachers. If the principal's dress is casual or sloppy, then the teachers and students will dress down from there. A principal wearing a suit and tie does not make one smarter. Dressing professionally sets a mood that we are serious about our profession. Some will argue that casual attire helps the children feel more comfortable with the teachers. Think about your doctor, dentist, banker, accountant, or stockbroker and their dress. You seek the best but would prefer those who dress the part as well. Would you feel comfortable with a doctor who wore a T-shirt, jeans, and tennis shoes? Educators should dress professionally every day. Encourage your staff to make sure their attire is neat, clean, and professional. Teachers in some areas such as physical education, art, and vocational technology will argue that they cannot wear "dress" clothes without ruining their clothes. I agree, but a person can still wear nice-looking collared shirts, appropriate pants, or sweats. Have discussions with your staff on dress guidelines in their areas. Some departments will purchase collared shirts with a school logo or department logo as part of their dress. This adds a nice touch to their teaching area. A second possibility is to purchase work aprons to help protect their clothing.

A common trend has been for organizations to adopt a casual Friday. Be careful with casual Fridays. Everyone has a different interpretation for what is appropriate. Casual Friday can turn out to be sloppy casual if you don't set guidelines. Some employees wear T-shirts that should be used to change the oil, denim jeans that have holes and tattered seams, stretched spandex and tight-fitting apparel, short skirts, sleeveless tops, and clothes that leave no imagination to the viewer. If you adopt a casual Friday, then set parameters for your employees. Again, the acceptable level becomes the highest level, and most will dress down from that level.

Smile

*No significant learning occurs without a
significant relationship.*

—Dr. James Comer

Get in the habit of smiling. Encourage your staff to smile. Frowning takes more muscles to use than a face with a smile. A smile can have a positive effect on your staff, students, and parents. It is the first step in developing a positive relationship. One year when my son Ty was in elementary school, we discussed the first day of school during dinner. We discussed the normal events of the day, and Ty expressed that his teacher really, really liked him. He knew that she liked him. My son's words were one of authority. It was an odd reflection for a child in primary grades. Most children will respond that their teacher is nice or funny or perhaps mean. I asked how he knew that his teacher liked him. Ty's response was that his teacher smiled at him 11 times during the day. It wasn't 10 or a bunch of times, but 11. Most people will use a round number or a nebulous number such as a bunch of times. My son had an accurate count. He counted the number of times that his teacher smiled at him during his first day of school. Wow! My son knew that he was going to have a great year because his teacher liked him. I wondered if the teacher actually smiled at him 11 times. She might have been looking at a funny-looking child. She might have been thinking about a funny episode from the day before. She might have been thinking about almost anything, but who cares? In my son's mind, the teacher was smiling at him. She really, really liked him. We both knew that he was going to have a great school year because a positive relationship had been started through a smile—11 smiles to be exact. In fact, he did have a great year. Ty became interested in his teacher, worshiped the ground she walked on, listened attentively, worked his tail off in class, and did everything possible to please her—all because of a smile.

Know Everybody's First Name

When you are good to others you are best to yourself.

—American Proverb

There are no great things, only small things with great love. Happy are those.

—Mother Teresa

Nothing is sweeter than the sound of your first name. Knowing everybody's first name is a simple thing that can spread goodwill to those you meet. Great leaders have an innate ability to memorize people's first names. Buy a memory book or take a class. Study the yearbook and place pictures and names together. Practice calling parents, students, and staff by their first names. If you don't remember or know a name, then ask the person, or ask another person to identify the person in question. Get in the habit of returning to the office and looking at your yearbook to figure out the name of a student or staff person. Knowing others' names makes people feel great. Part of everyone's mission should be to help others and make them feel good.

Develop Organizational Skills

An ounce of prevention is worth a pound of cure.

—Henry de Bracton

All leaders need good organizational skills. Take a few minutes every morning or evening to write a list of tasks you want to accomplish for the day. Check the list or cross off each task as it is accomplished. Consider using sticky notes to scribble a reminder during the day. Throw away the note when the task has been accomplished. Place a calendar on your desk with a list of meetings and deadlines for the week, month, or year. Technology allows leaders to put those same lists on their computers. I can recall when I was building a house that my father-in-law, Larry Brown, would continuously repeat, "Measure twice, cut once." He spent an enormous amount time on organization and preparation. This organization time helped save time when we began working because it decreased the number of mistakes. Time management is a concern for every leader. Every person has the same of amount of time each day. Learn to touch papers only once. You should react to the paper, file it, or throw it away. This habit will save you an enormous amount of time each day. My secretary, Becky Heil, has three clear folders on her desk specifically for me. One small 5 × 7 folder is for telephone messages. A second 8 × 12 folder contains FYI material. I am not expected to do anything with the items in this folder except read them. The third 8 × 12 folder is an action folder. I am expected to do something with the items in this folder. An item may require me doing something and returning it to the appropriate person. My secretary will place sticky notes next to places where my signature is required. She always makes copies of action papers before giving them to me. Accidents happen, but she always has a copy in the event I lose something or make a mistake on the original copy. Schools get an enormous amount of mail. My secretary saves me time by separating mail for me. Colored paper is another way to help save time. Certain colors represent people or topics. I quickly learned to recognize the topic by the color of the paper. My counselor, Jill Helfrich, loves to use florescent colors. I know it's from my counselor when I see the bright neon paper. A final thought is that a principal should always be prepared for the unexpected. Make plans for each possibility. Don't become too confident in your ability or position. History is full of upsets and unpredicted occurrences. Being prepared helps one to be proactive instead of a reactive leader.

Create a Support Group

The only way to have a friend is to be one.

—Ralph Waldo Emerson

No man is wise enough by himself.

—Titus Maccius Plautus

Create a plethora of friends, peers, and people you can count on to give support. Every leader needs a support system. Create a list of people you can call when faced with tough questions. It is easy to become too busy at school and lose contact with family and friends. Make it a regular habit to stay in contact and spend time with loved ones. It doesn't matter whether you call, e-mail, or write them, but keep in contact. Everybody needs somebody they trust to call for advice with important issues and challenges.

Eliminate Hoops

One thing you can't recycle is wasted time.

—Anonymous

If it were easy it would have been done before.

—Jeanne Yaeger

Resist the temptation to make your employees jump through hoops. Instruction is the most important part of the school day. Don't develop rules for the few who abuse things in your school. Conduct yearly staff meetings to discuss eliminating unnecessary burdens placed on your staff. Think of ways to reduce paper demands on your staff so they may concentrate on student learning in the classrooms. Often, bureaucracy increases as an organization grows. Leaders must learn to run a large school like a small school. Smaller schools tend to have less red tape and thus run faster and sleeker. As a school grows in numbers, more personnel are hired, and more rules are developed to run the school. Having worked in both a small district and a large district, I saw firsthand that school principals in smaller districts do it all. Right or wrong, they do it all. Customer satisfaction is about the same between small and large districts. Principals learn to rely on their building employees to help run the school. Large school districts may have several assistant superintendents, supervisors, directors, managers, and support personnel. Principals in larger school districts find they have more people helping them but may know less; and it may take longer for them to finish tasks as a result of the bureaucracy. Resist adding hoops for the employees. The principal needs to run a large school district like a fast and efficient small district.

No Surprises

Some things are so unexpected that no is prepared for them.

—Leo Rosten

Surprises are foolish things. The pleasure is not enhanced and the inconvenience is often considerable.

—Jane Austin

Encourage your staff to keep you informed. Stress that you want no surprises. Building trust takes time, but the dividends are worth it. Principals want employees to feel comfortable sharing information, including mistakes and concerns. No one is perfect. Mistakes happen, and it only makes it worse if someone tries to cover it up. My staff frequently lets me know small details in case a parent, central office employee, school board member, or community member calls me. I don't like surprises, and my staff knows this. I will remind my employees to keep me informed, so I will have an understanding of the situation and be able to assure people of the facts. In fact, my employees frequently say, "I don't want you to be surprised but...." Also, if I get a telephone call, and it seems that the person is upset, my secretary will sometimes take a message if she senses that I might be unaware of the situation. A few minutes allow me time to visit the teacher, get information, and gather my thoughts before I return the call.

Knowing a leader doesn't like surprises, make sure your bosses are not surprised, either. It doesn't mean that a principal should call the central office with every concern. Limit telephone calls to your superiors to major issues or concerns. Central office administrators don't want to be notified about every situation that happens in a school building. Learn to call with situations that could get worse or might catch someone off guard. A quick heads-up telephone call will suffice. Another possibility is to send an e-mail briefly explaining the situation, what you have done, and your plan of action. Let the central office know that you will take care of the situation but want to keep them informed. Furthermore, let the central office know that you will be in contact if anything changes or if you need their assistance.

Send School News to the Media

Perception can be reality.

—Unknown

Create a one-page media release template for your school employees. Keep it simple, including the headings *what*, *where*, *when*, and *who* on the page with a few lines underneath each heading. School information at the top of the template should include: school name, school contact person, school address, school telephone number, and school fax number. The template should include information for the media including the media contact person's name, address, telephone number, and fax number. The template should be created so staff can fill in the blanks with information pertaining to school events. The template should be simple as not to place another burden on staff. Staff should be able to complete the form in a few minutes. Encourage staff to submit school news reports weekly for you to fax to the newspaper or television network. Let the staff know that the media might only publicize 1 out of 20 events depending on how many schools are within that media area, so keep encouraging staff to submit classroom news, grade level news, department news, and schoolwide events. Principals and teachers need to let others know all the great things that are occurring in our schools. The school community won't know unless we tell them. Any positive news will help build a positive school perception with students, parents, businesses, and the community. A second reason to submit articles is that staff will reflect weekly on positive things happening in their classrooms, grade level, department, and school. It helps to remind us of the outstanding things we do each week. Third, it makes one wonder if a person, grade level, team, or department cannot think of anything spectacular each week, each month, each semester, each year. Nothing outstanding? It causes one to pause and reflect. Even great teachers who focus on teaching the standards with zeal and avoid extracurricular programs should have something to brag about. They should be able to share great student works.

Take Staff on Neighborhood Visits

The best time to be a friend is when you don't need a friend.

—African Proverb

Encourage staff to visit children in their homes and neighborhoods. A favorite ritual for principals is to rent a school bus for the entire faculty. They will take a trip visiting the neighborhood and children's homes. Seeing a student's environment will change your staff's perception. Frustrations for missing homework assignments, sleepy children, and unexplained student behaviors are bound to change the staff's feelings after visiting the neighborhood. Visiting neighborhoods help to keep things in perspective. Rita Pierson (2002) recommends that principals and staff have "drive bys," "go bys," and "stop bys." In a *drive by*, school employees drive around the neighborhood; they wave at people in the neighborhood, but they don't get out of the car. In a *go by*, school employees drive around the neighborhood; they stop the car, but they stay in the car as they talk to people in the neighborhood. In a *stop by*, school employees drive by the neighborhood, park at a student's house, and get out to talk to specific parents. School employees have to get out to the neighborhood, so people will know them. We don't want parents guessing who the principal or teachers might be. Parents are more accepting of any disciplinary actions you may take when they know you. It is imperative for principals to be seen in the neighborhoods.

Call Parents with Good News Early

Communication works for those who work at it.

—John Powell

Encourage your teachers to call parents the week before school starts or during the first week of school. The phone call can be a simple introduction, assuring the parents to call if they have questions, and telling them how excited you are to have their children in your classroom this year. Positive telephone calls early will help teachers who need to call parents later for assistance with a child's inappropriate behavior. Parents tend to be suspicious of teachers and principals who call home. They are used to receiving only bad news. Try calling and you'll be amazed at the parents' comments. After you introduce yourself and make a positive student comment, this will probably be followed with a pause on the other end of the telephone if you are not in the habit of making positive telephone calls. Some parents might even say, "But?" There is no "but"! You called to say something positive, that's all. Get teachers in the habit of calling early and often. It makes it easier for parents to digest negative news later on if the school has called 10 times before with positive news.

A key element to a successful teacher–student relationship is to have a positive teacher–parent relationship. Regular parent communication is paramount to a positive school relationship. Encourage teachers to send a weekly parent newsletter. Elementary teachers can send their own letter or one from the entire grade level. Secondary teachers could send a department or team newsletter. A one-page newsletter with basic information will suffice. A Web site that is updated weekly is another good source. Have regular telephone conversations. As students progress from kindergarten through the high school years, there is a tendency for school communication with parents to decrease. Great teachers learn to have regular parent communication. Most parents are willing to help if we communicate successes, concerns, opportunities, and class expectations. Parents have to know concerns exist before they can be expected to help. A leader does not want to hear the parent say, "If only I had known...."

Encourage Staff to Use a Variety of Procedures to Determine Student Progress

It's no fun being a genius when you are the only one who knows about it.

—Anonymous

The ways in which principals encourage less effective teachers to use a variety of procedures to determine student progress differ significantly from those for more effective teachers. Research found that principals supporting less effective teachers used a variety of procedures as opposed to principals supporting more risk taking and mistakes among more effective teachers (Fleck, 2003). It is interesting that principals want their less effective teachers to use a variety of procedures in the classroom but are not supportive of risks and mistakes. If principals expect teachers to develop innovative and creative lessons, then principals will have to support risks and mistakes. Not all students learn in the same way. Some are visual learners. Others are auditory learners. Some do better with hands-on learning. Encourage teachers to incorporate different teaching methods and modalities into their weekly routine. Also, ask your teachers what methods they use to determine student progress? Do students have different ways to show student progress? Do teachers use more than paper-and-pencil tests? Do teachers use portfolios? Writing assessments? Speaking opportunities? Projects? Collaboration assignments? Interdisciplinary assignments?

Encourage Teachers to Use Planning Periods on Instructional or School Duties

There are no gains without pains.

—Benjamin Franklin

An important task for the principal is student achievement and school improvement. Unfortunately, principals are spending an enormous amount of time in managing their less effective teachers. Encourage teachers to use their assigned planning time to call parents, document student behaviors, collaborate on team activities, and plan classroom activities. Research conducted found principals encouraging their less effective teachers, rather than their more effective teachers, to use planning periods on instructional planning or school duties (Fleck, 2003). Occasionally, teachers will use the planning period to relax, reflect, or attend to a personal issue. Don't let the occasional break become the habit. An assigned instructional period is a time to work on school-related activities. Many think that the contractual planning period is a time to do as they wish. It is not a time to conduct personal business or an entitlement to goof off every day. Great principals tend to be more relaxed with effective teachers than less effective teachers. The great teachers are doing their planning sometime during the day. It might be early before school or late at home. The less effective teachers need to be encouraged to use their time wisely to work during the assigned instructional planning period on school-related activities.

Encourage Staff to Write a Weekly Newsletter to Parents

It takes a village to raise a child.

—An African proverb

Encourage teachers to write a weekly newsletter to parents. It doesn't have to be major letter. It can be a newsletter from the individual teacher, an entire grade level, team, or department. Elementary teachers can send their own letter or one from the entire grade level. Secondary teachers could send a department or team newsletter. For example, seventh-grade teachers who are on a team could send one newsletter to parents. The newsletter would have information for each subject from that team of teachers. At the high school level the science department could send one newsletter with information in their respective areas. A one-page newsletter with basic information will suffice. Teachers could include a lunch menu, assignments, and special activities for the week. Encourage teachers to mention student accomplishments for the week. Parents and students enjoy reading students' names. Weekly newsletters help to keep parents informed and help them help their children. Schools need to do everything possible to get parents involved in their children's education. A principal may have to supply copies or a template for some teachers. The template can be saved and used again the next year. Only dates and minor changes would have to be corrected.

Write a Weekly Staff Newsletter

Think like a wise man but communicate in the language of the people.

—William Butler Yeats

Raise the Praise, Minimize the Criticize.

—Todd Whitaker

Write a weekly newsletter for staff. Be sure to include a weekly calendar of events and staff accomplishments. Keep employees informed of changes and upcoming events. Give details. Share information from each grade level, team, or department. A weekly newsletter allows staff to read information on their own and not waste valuable time in a faculty meeting going over logistics. Use the letter to praise staff. Everyone likes to hear praise and compliments. Todd and Beth Whitaker (1996) recommend a weekly staff memo that informs and organizes; motivates; shares staff development; announces public relations; and shares your philosophy, vision, and belief system.

Encourage Input

Ask advice, but use your common sense.

—American Proverb

The recipe for perpetual ignorance is: be satisfied with your opinions and content with your knowledge.

—Elbert Hubbard

Respect everyone's ideas and opinions. Too many consider the source of the idea before they embrace or reject it. Everyone has good ideas and thoughts. Great leaders learn to consider everyone's thoughts. Let staff know that you encourage input from everyone. This will encourage employees to share their bright ideas. Let staff know that you appreciate their efforts if the idea is not workable. The leader wants staff to continue thinking and sharing their ideas, good or bad. Employees are hesitant to share ideas and opinions with managers who practice a top-down style of leadership. A leader wants creativity to flow in their school.

Empower Staff to Act

As a manager, the important thing is not what happens when you are there but what happens when you are not there.

—Kenneth Blanchard and Robert Lorber

There can't be a crisis next week. My schedule is already full.

—Henry Kissinger

Leaders need to instill confidence in staff to act. Learn to give guidance without orders. Don't be the go-between on all decisions. A leader wants to train employees to think and react like the leader. A leader should constantly let employees know their beliefs, thoughts, and decision-making process. The greatest compliment to a leader is to hear the staff comment that they handled the situation the same way you would have.

Leaders have to trust that their employees will make good decisions. Leaders have to be careful not to create a leader-decision dependency with the staff. Administrators should not become crisis managers, where every decision has to be made by them. If you are going to be gone from the building, give words of encouragement to employees. With time, the staff will eventually say back to you, "We'll handle it. We always do. We'll be fine." If you are currently working on sensitive situations, give a recommendation or expectation in case that event occurs. Let the staff know that you will take care of the highly critical situations on your return. If a child is reprimanded or suspended by the building designee during your absence, your first comment on returning should be, "I know you would not have sent them home if you didn't think they needed to go." Principal comments are meant to build confidence and assure employees that they did the right thing. Employees will spread the message that they have a leader who supports staff decisions. Leaders want to empower their staff to act all the time, not just during their absences. Praising staff for good decisions will reinforce them to act accordingly in the future. Principals want to develop a culture where key leaders are empowered to act. Principals has to remember that part of their responsibility is training others to lead.

Learn What Parents and Students Want

One of the best ways to persuade others is with your ears.

—Dean Rusk

Keep abreast of what parents, students, teachers, community members, businesses, central office employees, and school board members want. Each group might want different results. Parents might want their children to receive a sound education while being treated fairly. Students may want challenging and engaging student lessons. Businesses might want trustworthy employees who are prepared to meet the demands of the future, who can write and speak using proper English, who are dependable, and who are team players. Central office employees may want high scores on state tests, a low suspension rate, and parent complaints held to a minimum. Pay close attention to each group's wants and revisit these wants regularly, because they may change each school year.

Give Messages
That Students Are Safe

Three billion people on the face on the earth go to bed hungry every night, but four billion go to bed every night hungry for a simple word of recognition and encouragement.

—Cavett Robert

Those in education have to convey messages to both students and parents that students will be cared for while at school. Encourage employees to send messages that the students will be taken care of. First impressions are very important. Parents should feel good leaving their children with us for the school day. Making parents feel at ease is challenging at times. A school's motto could be, "Not on my watch." This simple statement tells everyone that students will be taken care of while at school, and that all children will be safe until they get home.

The office secretary is the most important person in the school building. The secretary is the first and last person that students and parents meet when they visit a school. An opinion of the school environment is formed in those first few minutes with the secretary. A good secretary will dote over the family and make them feel good about coming to school. Parents calling the school will talk to the secretary first. An outstanding secretary can calm parents' fears and help send messages that their children are in good hands.

Teachers convey messages with telephone calls of good news to parents. Parents and students will more often accept a teacher correcting a student if the teacher has a habit of praising students. Taking the bad news is more acceptable when a teacher has sent home numerous notes of praise, made numerous telephone calls praising students, and praised students for their efforts.

Require the nurse to call parents when a child is sick or injured. Always call if in doubt about whether to call the parents concerning an illness or injury. Some parents can become upset if they are not notified by telephone.

The nurse calling parents sends a message that we are concerned about the safety of students. A bus driver conveys safety messages to parents and students when they enforce safety rules. A clean and well-kept building sends messages that safety is a priority. Disrepair, weeds, and a dirty building can make parents doubt whether their child will be taken care of while at school. Take pride in the appearance of the building and grounds. Spend time with the custodians and maintenance crew. Thank them for helping to keep the building and grounds looking great.

Encourage
Parent Involvement

Do not let what you cannot do interfere with what you can do.

—John Wooden

Be grateful for parents who involve themselves in their child's education. They can make your job so much easier.

—Jewish Proverb

Encourage parents to become involved in school activities. There are more things to do than working ball games and organizing fund-raisers. Parents can sell tickets or programs, read to children, tutor, serve as room parents, tend an adopt-a-garden-spot, paint, collate items, arrange bulletin boards and displays, videotape events, supervise lunches and halls, coach athletic and academic teams, and help supervise students at school events. Become creative and develop a list of wants and needs in your school. Encourage parents to be active leaders and participants in your school.

Organize
a Welcome Committee

A smile is a universal welcome.

—Max Eastman

Treat all visitors like royalty. The principal, secretary, and staff want to make a lasting impression that their school is the friendliest school in town. When visitors come to the school, use the student council to greet and meet your guests. Create a list of students from each homeroom who have the responsibility to come to the office and escort guests to their room. Set guidelines for the welcome committee. Have students practice, so they will be ready when guests arrive. Have them shake hands firmly, make eye contact, and introduce themselves. The welcoming committee representatives should be responsible for knowing general questions such as staff's names and the location of staff areas. Students and parents want to know how to find the cafeteria, gym, auditorium, media center, office, health center, counselor, and so forth. It makes a great impression on your guests, and it's wonderful public relations for your school. Use the same representatives to escort new students to their rooms, eat lunch with them, and escort them to each class. Have members of the welcoming committee meet new students before the parents leave school. Parents will be impressed and will be more at ease when they leave their children at the school. Feeling safe and secure is important for parents and students no matter what age.

Ensure that new employees are welcomed in the school. Don't assume that present employees will introduce themselves to new members of the school. Ask current employees to visit with new employees. Give a tour or ask an employee to give new faculty members a second tour. Make sure that new employees are always invited to luncheons. No one wants to start a new job and eat alone or feel isolated. A principal wants all students and employees to feel welcomed and a part of the school.

Requests
to Move Children
to Another Teacher

A child miseducated is a child lost.

—John F. Kennedy

Moving students to a different teacher can begin an avalanche of requests to move children. Moves can be related to the following examples: The teacher doesn't like my child; the teacher is too tough or too easy; friends are in a different class; male or female teacher; a desired teacher can relate better; a particular teacher had an older sibling; and so on. Several techniques can be used when a request occurs:

- Requests are honored.
- No requests are honored.
- Requests are honored if room permits.
- Requests are honored in rare exceptions.
- Requests are honored when put in writing.
- Only one request is honored during the student's entire school career at each level. For example, only one request would be honored during the student's K–5 years. The principal would have the parent and student agree to this in writing.

Principals need to learn how they will respond to teacher requests. If moving a child becomes part of your plan, then I would suggest that parents must meet with the teacher before any decision is made. Be prepared and learn to be tactful with parents.

Stress Procedures Early

Practice does not make perfect; perfect practice makes perfect.

—Vince Lombardi

Practice is everything.

—Periander

Encourage the staff to spend an enormous amount of time going over rules and procedures during the first few weeks of school. Teachers cannot focus on curriculum items until students are following procedures. Never assume that students and parents understand your expectations. The smallest and simplest detail is vital to having a successful year. For example, most elementary teachers emphasize the basics of quietly walking on the right side of the hallway, arms at their sides, eyes and heads forward, and not touching others. Great teachers go deeper and practice walking with students until they get it.

Potential trouble could be eliminated at the middle and high school level by practicing this rule. Consider a school where people do not walk to the right in the halls. Students could bump into each other, which could lead to pushing and possible fights. Students could become injured as they move from class to class between periods. Walking to the right helps to eliminate potential student conflicts and safety concerns. Don't assume that students will know this basic life courtesy.

Another example is the procedure for seeing the nurse. What if a student feels ill during a passing period? Does the student go to the nurse with a pass from the student's last teacher, the next teacher, or the office, or should the student just go without a pass? A lack of procedures could cause confusion. What if a fire drill occurred or the school had to be evacuated? Who would be responsible for the student? How would we know where the student was? Established clear procedures would help to ensure that the student would be safe with the nurse. Establishing procedures will help all grades. Consider procedures for bathroom needs, room needs, office needs, and teacher guidelines. Little things matter, and good teachers spend time on structure and classroom management early, so they can get to the important issues of curriculum.

Start the Year Sharing Expectations with the Entire Student Body

The world is full of abundance and opportunity, but far too many people come to the fountain of life with a sieve instead of a tank car or a teaspoon instead of a steam shovel. They expect little and as a result they get little.

—Ben Sweetland

It is time for us all to stand and cheer for the doer, the achiever—the one who recognizes the challenge and does something about it.

— Vince Lombardi

Students want and need to know the expectations of the principal. Start the year with an assembly that motivates students to perform well and shoot for the stars. Share school goals, successes, and areas for growth. Let students know that the school has the best teachers and the best students, and has a long history of performing well in academics and athletics. State expectations on attendance, student behavior, and student achievement. Motivate the students to be the best class ever. Take this opportunity to brag about their past successes. Express your dreams to make this year even better. Make sure every student gets to hear this message from both teachers and the principal. Be clear and concise, and think big. Students want to do well and will surprise you with great results.

Challenge Upper Grades to Accept Leadership Responsibility

I know God will not give me anything I can't handle. I just wish that he didn't trust me so much.

—Mother Teresa

Leaders should set expectations and challenge the uppermost grades to take leadership responsibility in the building. This could mean the seniors in high school, the eighth graders in middle school, and fifth graders in a K–5 building. Discuss modeling—older students helping younger students. Talk to older students about how younger students look up to them and how they set the tone—good or bad. Let the oldest students know that they are responsible for the environment in the school. Challenge these students to take active leadership roles and help you lead the school. Let students know that they are representing you, their parents, their school, their teachers, and, most important, themselves. Let the students know that your school has a history of high expectations, and express that you will be looking for them if something goes wrong. Also, explain that you wouldn't give them this responsibility if you didn't think they could handle it. Finally, instill confidence that you know the students will not disappoint you. Student leaders actively leading, modeling, and correcting inappropriate student behaviors will make your year go much smoother.

Be Visible Daily

You cannot know what you do not feel.

—Marya Mannes

The concept of "managing by walking around" was made famous in the best seller, *In Search of Excellence,* by Tom Peters (1982).

Leaders must be visible in the school and school community. Employees must see their leaders in the halls, cafeteria, and classrooms, at bus stops, and at school functions. Employees will feel that their leaders can relate better and are empathetic to their profession by being visible. This also provides opportunities for leaders to see any concerns firsthand. Seeing helps leaders understand and give direction to teachers and parents. Learn to lead from the trenches, not from the office.

It's powerful when you tell a parent that you personally observed their children in the classroom exhibiting certain behaviors, in contrast to relaying what the teacher said about the student. For example, think how powerful it is when you say, "I was in the classroom visiting and observed your child continuously talking and disrupting the lesson. The teacher tried to get your child involved in the lesson, by using many strategies to get your child engaged in the lesson. The classroom activity was excellent, but your child continued to disrupt the learning environment for the other children. Your child knew that I was in the room. Your child knows who I am but continued to disrupt the learning process. I only shudder to think what your child is doing when the principal is not in the classroom."

Being visible at potential trouble spots will reduce the number of students sent to the office. The presence of students in the office means more time spent doing paperwork and counseling students. While the principal is taking care of these problems, more potential problems could be occurring in the school. It can become a repeating sequence of the principal being trapped in the office, reacting to situations in the building, while yet more students' problems are occurring. It's never-ending.

Great leaders are visible at the hot spots and in the classrooms. Be a proactive principal, not a reactive principal. Also, it is too easy to get trapped in your office with deadlines and work that must be completed. A leader has to learn to do paper work in the early mornings and afternoons when students are not at school. It is important to lead others from the front, not from behind your desk. Teachers will follow the leaders' lead. Being visible sets a tone that being with the students is important.

Schedule Time
with New Employees

*We have enough people who tell it like it is—Now
we could use a few who tell it like it can be.*

—Robert Orben

Regular communication with all employees is important, but even more so with new staff. New employees will be reluctant to discuss concerns with you. An excellent strategy is to develop a regular time to meet with new employees. Have employees write goals. Goals could include both professional and personal goals. The goals should include short-term, immediate, and long-term goals. Sessions could be weekly in the beginning of the year, and biweekly or monthly during the second semester. Each employee is different, so you will need to schedule sessions depending on each employee's level. You want employees to succeed. Plan to informally discuss the employee's successes, challenges, and opportunities each session. Ask employees to reflect on their goals. New employees will look forward to discussing these three things if you establish a positive rapport. The principal must help new employees feel comfortable. No one is perfect. Experience is gained from both successes and mistakes. Developing trust takes time, so learn to use these sessions to build trust. The principal can help in this process by using paraphrasing techniques and helping the employees in reflecting on their own experiences. Resist the temptation to give quick answers. Instead, make each discussion a partnership of mutual sharing. Make each session an opportunity for both to share, with the lion's share from the employee.

Encourage Staff to Mentor Others

I expect to pass through life but once. If therefore, there be any kindness I can show, or any good thing I can do to any fellow being, let me do it now, and not defer or neglect it, as I shall not pass this way again.

—William Penn

McEwan's (1998) roster of "teacher-leader" activities includes mentoring, coaching, and collaborating with new staff. A principal has limited time and needs to create a climate where key leaders are mentoring and teaching other employees to help make the school more successful.

Todd Whitaker (1997) found that successful schools were able to identify and benefit from effective teachers. Learn to use the building's key leaders in leadership roles. Outstanding teachers will be able to share personal tips and management strategies, as well as identify potential pitfalls to avoid. The teachers in the building have a wealth of knowledge to share. Use them and their talents. Also, it's important to note that all teachers have talents and can share their experiences. Fleck (2003) found that principals encouraged more effective teachers (rather than less effective teachers) to mentor others. The principal needs to consider each person's strengths. Encourage all staff to share secrets of their talents and trade.

Help Staff Improve

Little by little does the trick.

—Abraham Lincoln

Create an environment that focuses on a continuous improvement model. Goals for student and staff improvement should be set yearly. Learn to revisit these goals during the year and reflect on successes and missed opportunities. Principals spend more time with less effective teachers on setting yearly goals and making more suggestions than with their more effective teachers (Fleck, 2003). Give guidance and support. Share research and best practices with staff. Cut out magazine articles. Online articles can be forwarded to staff. Discuss staff successes and growth opportunities. We tend to think that people outstanding in an area are highly motivated and don't want as many suggestions as ineffective persons. A principal should not assume that great teachers do not need or want input for improvement. Everyone, no matter how great, can use ideas for growth. An example of leadership adjustment is the coach who adjusts to a player. There is not one coaching style that works for all players. Good players might need very little direction, whereas less effective players may need more coaching from the coach—or leader. Each situation is different and calls for the principal to plan, respond, and lead depending on the situation and the personalities of employees. Law and Glover (2000) found that principals should use more of a coaching and directing leadership role when working with less effective teachers. The coach needs to consider the personalities of the team members and respond to their motivational needs. Outstanding employees need to improve as much as mediocre employees. Inspire your staff to stay current and be lifelong learners. Ubben and Hughes (1997) recommend that skill improvement should be in place for all members of the school and institute a vigorous program of education and self-improvement. Principals have to help teachers set improvement goals along with encouraging pursuit of professional development opportunities. Unfortunately, not all teachers perform at an acceptable level. Work with these teachers to improve their skills and make recommendations. Ask the teachers to make suggestions and develop an improvement plan. Have great teachers work with mediocre teachers. Use every possible means to help a teacher improve. To have great teachers, you can make the ones you have better or hire new ones. It's a whole lot easier to help make the ones you have better than to go through the process of removing them and hiring new ones.

Give
Educational Materials to Staff

None of the great discoveries was made by a "specialist" or a "researcher."

—Martin H. Fischer

Genius is one percent inspiration, ninety-nine percent perspiration.

—Thomas A. Edison

A leader should get into the habit of making copies of educational articles for the staff. Forward e-mails that have interesting tidbits and information. Give educational CDs, computer disks, magazines, books, and other programs that have been donated. Let the staff experiment with the program and give you feedback. Purchase inexpensive programs that look promising for your staff to further research. Leaders don't have time to thoroughly research every new program in school reform. Get in the habit of giving materials to your staff, and let them become a research lab for you. It might also stimulate some new thinking or reinforce instilled current practices. Anything to get your staff thinking about why they do or don't do things is good for your school.

Provide
Food and Refreshments

People are lonely because they build walls instead of bridges.

—Joseph Fort Newton

The best gifts are always tied to heart strings.

—Unknown

Food can have a motivational impact in education. Providing food, snacks, or refreshments will increase parent and staff attendance at meetings. Consider feeding your school community at special events to ensure their attendance. Provide refreshments at all teacher meetings. The little things go a long way in making others feel appreciated. Teachers will appreciate snacks and drinks after a long day as they spend time in a faculty meeting. Decorate the tables with bowls full of candy, fruit, or nutritional snacks. It doesn't always have to be a huge dinner. Cookies, candy, and fruit drinks are simple and inexpensive refreshments. Bring fruit and donuts on special occasions such as the first day of school, secretary's day, custodian's day, nurse's day, cafeteria worker's day, day-care workers day, teacher's day, and the last day of school. Encourage staff to take turns bringing goodies. Students love anything edible. Reward students with food if they reach achievement goals, make improvements, or meet expectations. Favorite goals usually focus on attendance, behavior, grades, improvement, and state testing assessments.

Support Efforts to Establish and Maintain Appropriate Student Behavior

Hold your head high, stick your chest out, you can make it.... It gets dark sometimes, but morning comes.... Keep hope alive.

—Jesse Jackson

Leadership is a two-way street, loyalty up and loyalty down. Respect for one's superiors; care for one's crew.

—Grace Murray Hopper

Everyone wants to feel as though they are supported. Superintendents want to feel supported by the school board. Central office employees want to feel supported by the superintendent. Principals want to feel supported by the central office employees. Assistant principals, teachers, and building employees want to feel supported by their principals. Leaders must support their leaders and their employees. Make every effort to support teachers to establish and maintain appropriate student behavior. A leader needs to establish a vision of appropriate student behavior and support the staff when they follow the principal's guidelines.

A principal must take over handling student discipline problems when staff has exhausted all possible means to correct inappropriate student behaviors. The question is: When has staff exhausted all means? A leader must establish a set of guidelines for the staff. Depending on the behavior, teachers should first handle all student concerns. Second, teachers should work with parents when no improvement occurs. Third, teachers should use support staff such as counselors, social workers, and assistant principals. Finally, the principal should take over for the rest of the staff. This also means that the principal is solely in charge of any consequences that may occur. Tell staff that once it's in your hands, you will dictate any punishments. Listen to teachers and parents for input, but keep in mind that any decisions are yours alone.

Eat Healthy and Exercise

Muscles are great. Everybody should have at least one that they can show off.

—Andy Warhol

Being a principal is hard work. It can consume your life if you let it. Don't neglect your health. Principals need to take care of themselves. Develop a regular exercise program and stick to it. It's better if you engage in a physical activity that you enjoy. Most experts will recommend that a person consider three things when developing an exercise program: frequency, duration, and intensity. Frequency is how often one exercises. For example, a person should exercise three times a week. Duration is how long one exercises; an example would be a person exercising for 45 minutes. Intensity is how hard one exercises. For example, a person jogging would have a higher intensity rate than a person walking. This means that a person might have to walk longer to reach the same intensity as a person jogging. An example when one puts frequency, duration, and intensity together is a person jogging three times a week for 45 minutes or a person walking four times a week for 1 hour. Be sure to make time to exercise weekly. A second healthy consideration for principals is to eat healthy. It can become too easy to eat on the go and late in the evening. Eat a healthy breakfast and lunch everyday. You will feel better, make better decisions, work longer, and live longer if you make time to exercise and eat healthy.

Don't neglect your body during the school day. A common habit of principals is to develop poor eating habits and skip exercising during the school year because they are too busy. Principals usually wait until summer to shed those extra pounds when they engage in an exercise program and start eating healthy again. Don't wait until summer. Consider forming an exercise group of fellow principals or teachers. The group will help to remind you that exercising is important and keep you actively engaged during the school year. Make eating healthy and exercising as important as any parent conference. Your students, parents, teachers, school, and family need you to be around for a long, long time.

Write Letters, Write Notes

Getting down to the nitty-gritty, most people are motivated by unconscious motives most of the time.

—Richard J. Mayer

Everyone likes to hear a compliment. Send letters and notes often. Write formal letters and save them on your computer. You can use these letters for special occasions. Send congratulatory letters that praise both the child and the parents. Write short notes of praise that are less formal.

Ben Bissell (1992) recommends five characteristics of effective praise: It is immediate, authentic, positive, specific, and private. To be more specific: (1) Send the note immediately. Don't be too long to tell them the good news. (2) Send only a positive note. Don't sandwich positive news around a concern. Keep it clean. (3) Keep the positive statement authentic. People don't want insincere praise. Make sure the person deserves the praise. Don't make up reasons to praise someone. (4) Give specifics. Don't give a general statement that says "you are doing a great job." People want details. (5) Mail the note or give it to the person in private. Unfortunately, some people are jealous and will sneer at others' accomplishments. Let the person being praised make the decision on whether to share their good news. For example, as a teacher, I set a goal to write two positive notes each period. Teaching six periods I was able to give 12 notes of praise a day. More notes were written on some days because my minimum goal was two notes per period. At the end of the period, I quickly wrote a note, folded it in half, and stapled it. I handed it quietly to students as they left for their next class; asking them to give it to their parents. Of course, the students would tear the note open, but I guarantee that the note made it home. Students had a choice whether or not to show it to other students. A checkmark in my grade book helped to remind me which students received notes during the grading period. Part of my goal was to make sure every student received several notes of praise every grading period. Principal notes to students could be rewritten or typed and mailed home. Another possibility is to give student notes of praise to their teachers. This gives teachers the opportunity to further praise the student as they hand deliver the note of praise from you. A principal should carry a notepad daily. Comment on positive things seen in the classrooms, cafeteria, offices, building, and grounds. You could place notes in employees' mailboxes when you return to the office.

2

During
the School Year

Have Regular Informal Conversations with Your Staff

Communication is a skill that you can learn. It's like riding a bicycle or typing. If you're willing to work at it, you can rapidly improve the quality of every part of your life.

—Brian Tracy

Leaders need to make sure that they have regular conversations with all of their employees. Make it part of your routine. Great principals make a habit of walking the halls daily and having short talks with the staff. The principal's daily mission is helping staff and students to be successful in their classrooms. Frequent informal conversations help the principal to keep a pulse on teachers' concerns and assist them when necessary. Informal discussions provide opportunities to share ideas and receive feedback. Staff ownership is strengthened when principals engage in communication that enables everyone to share and give their thoughts. Significant differences exist with principals who regularly have informal conversations with their staff. Principals have more informal conversations with their more effective staff as compared with their less effective staff (Fleck, 2003). Positive principal–teacher interactions were one of the factors associated with high-achieving schools (Shoemaker and Frazier, 1981). This is further supported by Bossert and colleagues (1982), who noted that highly effective schools appear to differ from less effective schools in terms of quality of human relations. There is a tendency to talk with favorite or effective employees in contrast to avoiding less effective employees. Make it a priority to talk with all employees.

Use Written and Verbal Communication to Help Employees Understand

The most important thing in communication is to hear what isn't being said.

—Peter Drucker

Research supports engaging as many of the senses as possible if you want the message to be retained. Learn to verbally tell staff news, followed by an e-mail or memo when conveying important messages. There are several reasons to use both written and verbal communication. Leaders should involve as many senses as possible. The staff gets to see and hear administrators. Also, verbal communication gives the principal an opportunity to see body language responses when conveying messages. An e-mail or memo may be sent following the conversation. A memo gives people the opportunity to see and read the written message at their leisure. In fact, they can read it again and again as they remember the verbal discussion (sight and memory). An administrator will never know if employees were completely listening when talking earlier. A written message tends to be clearer after having the opportunity to see a person's body language than a memo without a verbal discussion. What might be clear to one might not be clear to others. When using only written messages, educators have scratched their heads numerous times with the comment, "That's not what I meant." Reading a person's body language gives the principal the opportunity to clear up any misunderstandings. Using a written message alone does not allow an opportunity to read body language. A leader can only hope that the correct message will be received when using this form of communication.

Other means of communication include having both informal and formal conversations with people, involving people in the happenings of the school, developing ownership, and getting out of the office to see employees in their classrooms and areas. A good leader learns to make the time to visit people in their areas. Communicating face to face is an excellent excuse to get out of the office and see employees in their respective areas.

Keep
Written Messages Positive

Kindness consists in loving people more than they deserve.

—Joseph Joubert

Keep memos, letters, e-mails, and other forms of written communication positive. Principals need to be careful when writing something that could be construed as negative. Don't put anything negative in writing. A written document, memo, or e-mail is a permanent copy that can be kept, copied, and used against you forever. If you think there is the possibility that something will be interpreted negatively, then don't write it. The only exception would be a personnel reprimand that will be used in a paper trail to document unsatisfactory employee behavior. The principal should respond verbally, especially if the answer is " no" or bad news. A verbal message gives you the opportunity to read body language and see if your news is being interpreted correctly. It gives you the opportunity to explain your message. A written message can be interpreted in many ways that you did not wish, and once gone, it's gone. If parents, the community, or peers write you a nasty message, resist the temptation to respond. Call or talk to the person instead to clear up any misunderstandings. You, as the leader, will have the upper hand in this case because you have their negative note for your files, and they have nothing but their memories of your conversation. Keep in mind that a negative note will probably be shown to a wide network of people.

Think Time

Leaders of the high-performing companies communicate their vision in their daily actions. The best testament is the living testament.

—James A. Belasco

Time is an illusion, lunchtime doubly so.

—Douglas Adams

Arriving early and leaving later allows more uninterrupted time to do paperwork. A principal should be too busy working with teachers, visiting classrooms, helping students, and meeting parents to do paperwork during students' hours. Arriving early and leaving late allows you time to think and work uninterrupted. Trying to do paperwork during school hours is fruitless. An enormous number of interruptions will occur, so why try? A common question asked of a principal is, "May I interrupt you for a second?" That usually means it will take 10 minutes or more, plus the time to regroup your thoughts where you left off before the interruption. Make the best use of your time; do paperwork before students arrive and after they leave for the day. A leader needs to be a positive role model in the building. Also, arriving early and staying late can serve as an inspiration for employees. This time-management strategy shows employees that teachers and students are more important than paperwork.

Staff Success
Means School Success

A basic rule for managers is "Pass the pride down." People like to create when they can earn recognition for their ideas. When a good idea surfaces, the creator's immediate superiors should show prompt appreciation.

—James L. Hayes

A leader's duty is to make sure that all employees are successful. The leader has to make it a daily mission to help teachers with their daily concerns. If teachers and building employees are successful, then the students will be successful. School success is directly dependent on students being successful. Start each day reflecting on the previous day's concerns. Consider: Who needs my assistance? What occurred the previous day that needs to be addressed? What can I do to help my staff and students succeed? Am I doing anything that inhibits staff or students from succeeding? Who needs their efforts affirmed? Make it a daily mission to support employees so they can help the students be successful. When the employees are successful, then the students, school, and principal will be successful.

Be Positive

Act enthusiastic and you become enthusiastic.

—Dale Carnegie

One study found that people are engaged in some sort of negative thought more than 70 percent of the time. A leader needs to be aware of negativity and look for positive things happening in the building everyday. It's crucial for the leader to be positive. Success is an attitude. Focus on what you have control over instead of what you do not have control over. Look for ways to point out teacher and student positives every day. The payoff will be a more positive climate and environment. Everyone likes to hear kind words of praise and encouragement. This doesn't mean insincere flattery, but sincere remarks that show you appreciate them. Learn to praise their accomplishments to others, especially in their presence. Writing letters to students, parents, and staff is a perfect opportunity for praise. Write letters that praise parents for students' successes. Parents love reading a letter from the principal thanking them for their hard work in raising an outstanding child.

A leader cannot have too many bad days. Teachers, staff, and students follow your mood. If the leader is in a foul mood, then the teachers will most likely be in a foul mood, followed by the students being in a foul mood. It's a high probability that your office will fill up with office referrals and students if you have a poor disposition. Excellent leaders learn to fake it. Be positive and look for the sunny side every day. It's important that the teachers and students are in a good mood so they can concentrate on learning. A favorite habit is to greet staff as they sign in and prepare for the day. I don't do anything special except to say something positive. My motive is to have staff in a positive frame of mind.

Next, I greet students with a bright smile and say hello as they enter the building. Again, we want our students to be in a positive mood. Greeting students as they enter school or are dropped off from the bus allows you to see students who are in a bad mood. You want to get these students in a positive frame of mind. You can read a person's body language and hopefully help them with their problems. It's important to eliminate potential problems before they become bigger problems. Bad moods are contagious. Walk the halls early when students are at their lockers; greeting staff and students provides an opportunity to set the tone that this will be great day. It doesn't take much effort on your part: just a smile, a compliment, or a kind word that the day will be wonderful.

Presume Positive Intentions

If you look for the bad in mankind expecting to find it, you surely will.

—Abraham Lincoln

Always presume positive intentions when dealing with people. Educators need to give the benefit of doubt and consider that a person's action is positive. Resist the temptation to jump to conclusions. Don't assume that you know the facts as you may be wrong. For example, if employees are whispering with each other during a meeting or presentation then assume that the employees might be engaging in dialogue that corresponds with your topic. This same example would apply to students talking during a teacher's lesson. You may want to discuss expectations with the parties following the meeting. Seek to understand. Gather information before you redirect a person who is making poor choices. In contrast, if you condemn first and find out that the person's intent was positive then it's too late to take back your comments. You can say you're sorry but the relationship might be strained. We want to have a positive trusting relationship. You might think that you know what is going on but you could be wrong. Making a poor choice could be a lack of understanding. It is the leader's responsibility to make sure that everyone understands expectations. Consider the following: If a teacher or student is sick, do you or your staff make disparaging remarks? If a person or student is late to school, do you raise your eyebrows when they give their reason? If an employee is accused of misconduct, do you assume that the complaint is plausible or do you ask questions to further understanding? Consider the classroom that is loud, a teacher who sends a student to the office, or is late with an assignment. Don't assume that the teacher lacks classroom management or is unorganized. Inquire before condemning their behavior. If a student is running in the halls, at the scene of a fight, or with another student who is in trouble; do you listen, gather facts, and assume that there is a good reason for their behavior or do you presume that they are guilty. Consider parents who are behind in school payments, miss appointments, or provide excuses for their child's behavior. They might be telling the truth even if they have a history of false promises. Always give yourself an out. Assume that people's actions are positive. Make people prove you wrong.

Keep No Secrets
from Your Staff

The best thing to invest in now is collegiality. The number one skill that teachers will need is to be team-based, collegial, sharing their knowledge and wisdom.

—Alan November

Education in the past has been too much inspiration and too little information.

—E. Franklin Frazier

Share information with all employees. Significant differences existed with principals when sharing information on school issues with their staff. Principals shared more information with their perceived effective staff than with their ineffective staff (Fleck, 2003). Everyone wants to feel as though they are a part of the school. Sharing information helps to build a positive climate and school environment. Leaders need to be aware that there is tendency to communicate school news with more effective school employees and limit sharing information with less effective employees. Some leaders try to keep information from their staff. Leaders make comments such as, "It's confidential." or "You're on a need-to-know basis." With very few exceptions, such as employee personnel issues, there is no reason to keep secrets from employees, especially when the information concerns the students. A school is a team working together, and every little piece of information might help a student or overcome challenges within the school. Become a leader who is constantly sharing information with your staff. Leaders don't have all of the answers, and sharing information with all employees allows them the opportunity to become a part of the problem-solving team. Sharing student information is like doing a puzzle. It takes all of the pieces to see the entire picture. Even some small, irrelevant piece of information might make sense to the school team at a later date. School employees are on the same team, and every person needs to have the same information. Leaders need to reassure the staff that there are very few exceptions to keeping secrets. Remind your employees, "If I know, you'll know."

Practice Speaking

Good communication is as stimulating as black coffee, and just as hard to sleep after.

—Ann Morrow Lindbergh

Leaders are expected to master the art of speaking. Very few feel comfortable speaking before others. Take advantage of opportunities to speak before others with short speeches and gradually move to longer speeches and larger crowds. Experience and confidence in yourself and subject are the keys. Prepare your speech in advance. The better you know your subject, the more confidence you will have in speaking about the subject. Outline the main points and then fill in details as you prepare your speech. Consider your audience. What is the point of your speech? What do you want your audience to do after they receive your information? Don't try to memorize too much information, especially new information. Too much new information can add to your nervousness and cause confusion. Keep everything simple and practice, practice, practice. Consider joining a speaker's organization. Videotape yourself or record your speeches. Study your body language and listen to your message. Eliminate unwanted words, pauses, and body movements. Take advantage of speaking at church, youth organizations, and community clubs. Speaking with students in small groups and at assemblies is an excellent way to gain confidence and experience.

Use Correct Grammar

There may be no single thing more important in our efforts to achieve meaningful work and fulfilling relationships than to learn to practice the art of communication.

—Max De Pree

Educators must take care to speak and write using proper syntax and grammar. Those in education, especially leaders, will be expected to speak and write properly without mistakes. Spelling and grammar checkers on computers have made it easier, but computers don't catch everything. Get in the habit of proofreading memos. A writing program will catch simple mistakes before sending e-mails and notes. Copying and pasting the message to an e-mail is simple. Notes can be copied from the computer screen. The larger the group that receives written messages, the more proofreaders that should be used before sending it out. My friend Tom Johnson shared that his boss Phillip Schlechty, founder of Schlechty Center for School Leadership, set the bar high for written correspondence. All employees are to have zero spelling and grammar mistakes on all written correspondence. To have 100% correct is an outstanding goal, a goal that every educator should strive for. The secretary and principal can work together, reading each other's work, thereby increasing the odds of getting 100% correct.

Speaking before groups is more difficult. It takes practice. Keep your message simple and use simple words until you gain experience. Nervousness can cause mistakes when speaking before groups. Practice, practice, practice! Take the time to practice in your office, auditorium, home, car, and other settings before the actual performance. Learn to write answers to media questions before the reporters arrive. If something happens in the community or at school, write down questions that you may expect to be asked, and practice answering those questions before reporters arrive. Employees, parents, students, and the public expect you to model proper English usage. Grammatical mistakes taint your message because listeners will focus on them. Good communication is a must to succeed.

Eye Contact

Good manners will open doors that the best education cannot.

—Clarence Thomas

Make eye contact when speaking to students, teachers, and parents. Resist the temptation to look at your to-do list, down the hall, or past the person. If you are buried in paperwork at your desk, then stop and look directly at the person speaking to you. If you are at the computer, stop typing, get up, and establish eye contact. People will remember how they were treated.

A principal made a lasting impression on the importance of eye contact with me. Poking my head into Debra Harrington's office, I could see she was buried in paperwork. She looked up at me, and I responded that I could see she was busy and I would return later. She pushed the mound of paperwork to the side, folded her hands, and asked what she could do for me. This principal treated me like I was the most important person in the world. It didn't stop there. Mrs. Harrington didn't respond until I was finished speaking. As a teacher, I was used to speaking extremely fast to administrators because I had been trained to get everything out before the principal said "no." Mrs. Harrington was different. She didn't interrupt, so my speaking speed got slower and slower. She might have been thinking about other things, but it didn't matter because she focused on me during our conversation. I felt extremely important when I left that day.

In contrast, a fellow principal told an embarrassing story. He was at his desk working when a teacher came into the office and asked if he was busy. He said "no" and told the teacher to come in. As the teacher spoke, the principal continued writing at his desk. Eventually the teacher said, "You're busy. I'll return when you have time for me." This principal was embarrassed, but he confessed it was the best thing that happened to him. He wondered how many others he had treated rudely, who lacked the courage to say something to him.

Maintaining eye contact can be difficult when you have a busy day, but it's the way we want to be treated. Eye contact can make students, parents, and teachers feel like the most important people in the world at that present moment. Learn to look people in the eye, shake hands, and repeat their names. Repeating a person's first name helps to place it in your memory banks. Too often people will forget a person's name as soon as they are introduced. Repeating the name helps to imprint it in your mind.

Don't Talk When Someone Else is Talking during Meetings or Presentations

Children have more need of models than of critics.

—Joseph Joubert

As a leader or a manager in your organization, you must start to behave in a manner that is congruent with the behavior you expect from your employees. The top managers in any organization must model the behavior they desire for the rest of the company.

—Karl Albrecht

Be a positive role model. It's rude behavior to talk when someone else is talking. Also, don't do paperwork or grade papers during a presentation. A common annoyance for teachers are students who are not listening in class, talking during their lesson, or working on another assignment. We don't like it. Learn to listen to others who are speaking. Be respectful of their feelings. Leaders have to model appropriate behavior for their staff.

If this is a concern, then consider establishing norms for meetings. Norms could include: turning cell phones off, not working on your laptop computer, not grading papers, starting and ending times, and rules for talking.

Telephone Etiquette

That best portion of a good man's life, his little, nameless, unremembered acts of kindness and of love.

—William Wordsworth

Good manners are made up of petty sacrifices.

—Ralph Waldo Emerson

Teach and expect your staff to always answer the phone in a polite and professional manner. A leader might have to write it down and even model it for others, especially if you have student office workers. It is an important skill that makes others feels good about the school. It is appropriate to answer the telephone with a greeting, followed by the school's name, your identification, and asking how you may help them. For example, "Hello, Welcome to Glenwood Middle School, This is the principal, Sheila Huff. How may I help you?" It is recommended that you smile when speaking on the telephone. It might seem ridiculous to flash a smile that no one can see, but smiling will subconsciously improve your mood. Smiling will increase your positive thoughts and enthusiasm, which will be transmitted with a more positive tone and choice words.

Approve Memos to Parents

Say all you have to say in the fewest possible words, or your reader will be sure to skip them; and in the plainest possible words or he will certainly misunderstand them.

—John Ruskin

Miller (2001) reported, "Until principals can significantly reduce the time they spend on parent concerns and other noninstructional management issues imploring them to engage in more instructional leadership will do little." Research has found that principals read parent correspondence of their less effective teachers more than that of their more effective teachers (Fleck, 2003). Even though it takes time for principals to read parent correspondence from their less effective teachers, it is an opportunity to help teach and train them in the art of tact. Principals will find that, with time, these teachers will learn how to write tactful yet specific letters that help parents help their children. It only takes one negative letter to damage a teacher, principal, or school reputation. Letters are unlike face-to-face correspondence because parents will have the copy for life. Also, they have the copy to show to family, friends, and neighbors. At least with oral communication, you can read body language and make adjustments if your information is being perceived negatively. Principals only have so much time in a day, but it should be time well spent. Hopefully, this time-management task will decrease as less effective teachers become better writers. Trust and experience is the key.

Respect Everyone

Civilization is a method of living, an attitude of equal respect for all men.

—Jane Addams

Knowing is not enough; we must apply. Willing is not enough; we must do.

—Johann Von Goethe

Show respect to all. The Golden Rule applies no matter where or who you are. Treat others as you would want to be treated. Every day provides us an opportunity to show others how to properly behave, speak, and act. This means letting others go first and opening doors for others, saying "thank you" and "please," and showing respect when others have shown rudeness. A person's age, intelligence, social economic background, political clout, or viewpoint should not matter in regard to being respectful. It shouldn't matter who you are, who you know, or what you do. Treat everyone with respect. People will remember kindness as well as rudeness.

For some of our students, school is the best part of their day. We have no idea who and what environment our students go home to every day. Our students need us more than ever, especially when some exhibit undesired behaviors and use inappropriate language. This makes it all the more important to model appropriate behavior and to serve as positive role models.

Express Thanks and Send Thank-You Notes

All doors open to courtesy.

—Thomas Fuller

Manners are stronger than laws.

—Thomas Carlyle

Learn etiquette rules. Always say "thank you" and "please." Purchase a book on proper etiquette and manners. A leader must model appropriate behavior at all times. Actions are more important than words. Learn the social rules.

Always thank guests for visiting as they leave your building. Make a point to show your appreciation for their visit and remind them to visit often. The leader needs to thank guests and serve as the role model for their building. For example, get in the habit saying, "Thank you for visiting Dexter Elementary. I hoped you enjoyed your visit. Don't be a stranger. You're always welcome. Come again soon." If you send thank-you notes, send them as soon as guests leave or on returning from visiting them. Provide compliments and appreciation in your note. If possible, be specific in your note of appreciation.

Become Interested in Your Employees' Families

There is a great man who makes very many feel small. But the real great man is the man who makes every man feel great.

—G. K. Chesterton

A compliment is verbal sunshine.

—Robert Orben

Get in the habit of learning details of every employee and family. If necessary, write down the names of their family and important details that pertain to them. Occasionally, ask questions that pertain to their family. A family is the most important thing in their life. Asking sincere questions makes people feel great. Leaders should take an interest in their employees and their lives. Employees should be treated as more than employees; they are family.

Overdeliver

Hold yourself responsible for a higher standard than anybody expects of you. Never excuse yourself.

—Henry Ward Beecher

Actions lie louder than words.

—Carolyn Wells

Always do more than is required of you. Too many settle for doing the minimum. Go the extra mile and always give more. The difference between average and being the best is a small difference of time. Make it a priority to be the best. Instill an attitude to give a little bit more. Learn to underestimate and overdeliver. Always promise what you think you can do, but always give more than promised. People are pleasantly surprised when expectations are exceeded.

Consider Staff Opinions When Making Decisions

The best way to get a good idea is to get a lot of ideas.

—Linus Pauling

Great principals learn to consult with as many stakeholders as possible before issuing a plan. Learn to increase the amount of input from stakeholders as the importance of a decision increases. If the importance of the decision decreases, then possibly decrease the amount of input from stakeholders. Be careful decreasing the amount of input from stakeholders. Something that you consider a minor decision could be considered major to others. It's still a good habit to consult. All people can add valuable information to a plan or decision. A favorite technique is to have a list of dependable individuals who are representative of the stakeholders. Talk to these individuals to get a quick pulse on your ideas. Another method is to develop ownership in the plan. People want to feel as though they have had input in the decision. Principals should use a collaborative, shared decision-making approach with teachers and place an emphasis on teacher empowerment (Leithwood, 1992b). Teachers must be included in planning and making decisions with the principal if schools are to meet the increasing demands placed on schools. A principal improves their chances of making a better decision when the number of employees sharing opinions increases. Research shows that principals considered the opinions of their effective staff more than their ineffective staff when making decisions (Fleck, 2003). Everyone has ideas and should be able to share their views. Learn to ask all employees for their thoughts. Don't get in the habit of asking the same people or only a few individuals. Even worse is to make the decision alone without any input. The more people who share opinions, the more improved chance of success. Also, staff members sharing their opinions helps to build ownership in building-level decisions. Everyone wants to feel as though they are a part of the team. Whitaker and Valentine (1993) determined that effective schools were able to identify and involve effective teachers in making decisions. Ask for staff input and opinions when making decisions. Employees are more likely to embrace decisions when they feel they have been a part of the decision-making process. In contrast, employees may revolt or sabotage plans if they feel they are powerless in the decision-making process. *Doers* of plans should be the *planners*. As principal, you need to think how you will include input from all employees. What avenues will you use for staff input? How will you use and involve teachers in decision making?

Use a Problem-Solving Approach When Making Decisions

When solving problems, dig at the roots instead of just hacking at the leaves.

—Anthony J. D'Angelo

Ability is the art of getting credit for all of the homeruns somebody else hits.

—Casey Stengel

Develop a problem-solving approach. If your school has a problem, there is probably something you all can do to make it work better. Sometimes it takes a couple of heads working together to find a good solution. Brainstorming with a small group will help. E-mailing the staff to ask them to respond with their thoughts is a quick way to poll and receive staff perspectives. You're not asking for a vote, you are requesting input from the staff. You might get a small sampling of responses, but your staff will have had an opportunity to respond. Often, it will help you look smarter. Employees will ask, "Did you think of. . . ?" It's amazing.

A leader wants to avoid retracting a decision if possible. It's embarrassing to make a decision and have to retract it immediately. Staff input helps the principal eliminate the, "I didn't think about that." Another reason to e-mail the staff is to develop ownership in your building decision-making. A major employee complaint is to feel as though they have no input. This gives all employees the opportunity to share. When faced with a decision, gather as much data as possible from as many sources as possible. This can mean exploring the Internet; reading books, articles, and magazines; and discussing with peers, universities, employees, parents, students, businesses, and community members before considering your options. Leaders need to consider the options and consequences of each decision. Consider the risks with each decision. Make sure your decisions are consistent with your vision, goals, and objectives. Consider the talents of your employees. Match employees with the objectives wanted. Communicate those plans. Evaluate the plan. One possibility is to create a diverse school group that the leader can quickly poll when faced with a concern that needs a quick answer. The group may give valuable input to help you when faced with decisions.

Never Leave
Today's Work for Tomorrow

*Work while you have the light. You are responsible
for the talent that has been entrusted to you.*

—Henri-Frédéric Amiel

*We expect our leaders to be better than we are. . .
and they should be—or why are we following
them?*

—Paul Harvey

Learn to do all that you can each day because the next day is full of tasks. Organized administrators will do what they can each day and then go home knowing that they did their best. Resist the temptation to move today's tasks to tomorrow. Learn to handle the unpleasant tasks first to get them off your list, unless you need more time to ponder your course of action. Doing unpleasant jobs first makes the rest of the day seem brighter. In contrast, keeping an unpleasant task for the end of day makes one dread the entire day.

Doing Well
Is What Matters Most

Blessed is he that expects nothing, for he shall never be disappointed.

—Benjamin Franklin

No one should teach who is not in love with teaching.

—Margaret E. Sangster

We are in the people business to help others, not for personal rewards. Spend each day using your talents to serve others. Looking for rewards and recognition is not the reason to help others or do a good job. Doing what's right and a good job should be our purpose in life. Benjamin Franklin started each day saying, "What good will I do today?" At the end of his day, he asked, "What good did I do today?" My wife and best friend, Kristy Fleck, ends each evening with the thought, "Lord, help me do something tomorrow that makes you proud of me."

Stay Calm

The foundations of character are built not by lecture, but by bricks of good example, laid day by day.

—Leo B. Blessing

A leader must be a calm individual when any concern arises; a rock that others look to during a time of crisis. Mayor Rudolf Guiliani and President George W. Bush were remarkable in their ability to remain calm during the events of 9/11. Their calmness instilled confidence that all would be well during the emergency. Teachers, students, and parents will follow the lead of their leader. If the leader panics, then others will too. The principal might be scared to death inside but must not panic. You may have to fake it. Being proactive can help. Think of situations that might occur and think how you should respond during the situation. Write it down and file it away so you can refer to it in case that situation might occur. Discuss possible situations in staff meetings or with selected staff members who would be involved in various situations. It is better to be prepared than sorry. Losing your temper is another behavior to curb. Others will follow your lead. If you yell at the students, then they will be sure to do likewise. If possible, keep a calm demeanor at all times.

Don't Rush a Decision

A few observations and much reasoning lead to error; many observations and a little reasoning lead to truth.

—Alexis Carrel

Great leaders learn to think before acting. Take time to observe, reflect, probe, investigate, question, and listen before jumping to conclusions. Everything is not always as it seems. Take the time to thoroughly investigate a situation before you take action. What might seem plausible might be different in reality. A common pitfall is to rush a decision. You may have a messy desk, a busy schedule, and a long list of tasks before you. Make sure to have the facts. Think about what is the best decision before acting. Consider how people will respond to your decision before you act. Once you make a decision and communicate the plans, it's too late take back what you said. You can always change your decision, but it's embarrassing and can cause groups to lose faith with you. If you aren't sure your decision is right, then sleep on it and make a decision the next day. If groups are pressuring you for a decision, then let them know that you want to thoroughly investigate the matter before making a decision. You might consider giving a time and date when you think you will have a decision. If you give a timeline, then make sure to let groups know by that designated time. It is better to put off a decision for a day then to make a hasty decision that you could regret.

Don't Make Decisions to Keep Friends

I don't know the key to success, but the key to failure is trying to please everybody.

—Bill Cosby

People may doubt what you say but they will believe what you do.

—Anonymous

Principals are setting themselves up for failure if their goal is to get everyone to like them. A leader will avoid making tough decisions because of fear of upsetting their friends. Leadership is not a popularity contest. The leader needs to make decisions based on what's best for the students and the school, not for political reasons or friendships. Let staff know it's not personal, it's business.

Build Allies

We must always seek to ally ourselves with that part of the enemy that knows what is right.

—Mahatma Gandhi

Power consists in one's capacity to link his will with the purpose of others, to lead by reason and a gift of cooperation.

—Woodrow Wilson

Having different opinions is part of life. Leaders understand that others' thoughts will differ from theirs. The difference between great and mediocre leaders is that they will limit the number of permanent enemies when they disagree with people. You can always agree to disagree but work to keep a respectful relationship. A permanent enemy will be a thorn in your side. It is important to remember that having permanent enemies means that their friends, families, and followers will be your enemies, too. Endeavor to build a relationship of respect, especially when you disagree. Life is too short to be constantly battling during the school year.

A leader needs to do more than dictate. Collaboration is a skill, but it cannot be used all the time. Someone who tries to please everyone will fail, but a leader can work to make allies of their subordinates through many different means. It takes time to build relationships and allies. Learn to have daily conversations with your employees, students, and parents. Learn their likes, dislikes, and concerns, and nurture those relationships religiously. If a leader has to make a tough decision, then subordinates are less likely to rebel if you have earned their respect. Take the time now to build allies in case that rainy day comes. Also, employees will respect you more if you personally tell them that you made a decision that they did not agree with. Employees might not like your decision, but when you tell them face to face, you will build trust and respect. Personally telling employees about a decision sends the message that you cherish their approval and respect their opinions, and it bothers you to do something that they don't agree with. A leader has to develop positive interpersonal relationships.

Learn to Collaborate

A person is silly who will not take anyone's advice, but a person is ignorant who takes everyone's advice.

—Anonymous

We must learn to live together as brothers or perish together as fools.

—Dr. Martin Luther King Jr.

Collaboration should be everyone's first choice. Leaders learn to collaborate with all stakeholders and instill an ownership in the organization's decision. Occasionally, leaders will have to dictate a decision. Dictating should be used as a last resort. A professor of mine once said, "The view of a 1,000 asses is still the view of an ass." This quote was not to put us in shock. The professor wanted us to make a good decision based on good information, in contrast to making a decision based on what the majority wants.

Sometimes the majority can be wrong based on special interests. A leader has to collaborate with others but make sure to seek information from a diverse group before making a decision. Consider what each group wants, the liabilities of each decision, and the positives of each decision.

Don't Wait
for Group Consensus

Get action. Seize the moment. Man was never intended to become an oyster.

—Theodore Roosevelt

Carpe diem, quam minimum credula postero.

—Horace

There will be times when opportunities present themselves for the leader to seize the initiative, make a decision, and move full speed ahead. The leader must take full advantage of these opportunities, move quickly, and use your power if necessary. A leader doesn't always have to collaborate. It might mean that the principal becomes a committee of one. If something good for the school community presents itself, then act. The staff will accept occasional autocratic leadership so long as there is a high level of trust. Besides, if the principal has been doing a good job of communicating, having frequent discussions, and building positive relationships with staff, the principal will know how employees feel.

Be Consistent

Do all the good you can, by all the means you can,
in all the ways you can, in all the places you can,
at all the times you can, to all the people you can,
as long as ever you can.

—John Wesley

Students, parents, and teachers may expect you to do the same thing every time for every situation. It's difficult to do the same thing, every time, and the same way. Every situation is different. It is more important to be consistently fair. When I was a first-year assistant principal, Principals Jack Woods and Jim Mason gave me the advice, "We will treat everyone the same, only differently." This bit of wisdom reminded me to be consistent by being fair to each person and considering each situation. There is not a cookie-cutter approach to every situation. If there were, then you wouldn't need administrators. You could look up the answer to a situation in a book and follow the recipe. In education, every situation is different. It's not black or white. It's gray. The key to running an organization is consistently being fair and doing what's right.

No Whining

Realize that if you have time to whine and complain about something then you have the time to do something about it.

—Anthony J. D'Angelo

Don't find fault. Find a remedy.

—Henry Ford

Resist the temptation to complain or whine. Keep a positive attitude no matter how bad the day. Teachers and students need to see us in a positive mood. Success is an attitude. Develop an attitude that you will overcome all obstacles. Develop an attitude to focus on what you have control over instead of focusing on what you do not have control over. It is important for us to think and be positive. Complaining serves very little purpose. It usually drags you and others down. Let others know that your school does not allow whining. Put your efforts toward solving concerns.

Use Persuasion

We are generally the better persuaded by the reasons we discover ourselves than by those given to us by others.

—Blaise Pascal

Tact is the art of convincing people that they know more than you do.

—Raymond Mortimer

It is better to persuade others than to dictate an order. Developing owner-ship in a decision is important. Success rates are more likely to increase as ownership in the decisions increase. Leaders want employees to believe that the idea was theirs in the first place. Take great pains to ensure that employ-ees believe that plans started and ended with them. Remember, the doers should be the planners. Principals want employees involved in the decision making of the school. It will increase the success rate of any plan or program. People who feel as though the idea was theirs are more likely to make it work. It's a mindset that will make it happen: This is a great idea, and I will ensure its success. Then the plan will not fail. Principals want employees spending their efforts on developing, supporting, and leading initiatives in the schools. Leaders may occasionally have to dictate orders, but persuasion is always a better method.

Trust is My Most Valued Asset

Honesty means integrity in everything. Honesty means wholeness, completeness; it means truth in everything—in deed and in word.

—Orison Swett Marden

Oh, what a tangled web we weave,
When first we practice to deceive!

—Sir Walter Scott

Trust is a leader's most valued asset. Principals can have disagreements, differences of opinions, and even bitter fights with people, but they must always be honest. That doesn't mean that you have to tell parents, "I agree that Mrs. Smith is a lousy teacher." It can mean that you acknowledge their concerns and address them. We have to have trust. As trust levels go up, the level of intolerance decreases. As trust levels decrease, intolerance increases. If people trust you, they won't be spending as much time focused on your decisions. Leaders want a high level of trust so that employees, parents, and community stakeholders will spend their efforts on more constructive endeavors. I have seen groups bombard school board meetings because of perceived acts of mistrust. This may cause administrators to spend an enormous amount of time explaining their decisions. Keep trust levels high with all groups of the community so you can focus your strength and efforts on school improvement and student achievement.

Help Others Succeed

Everybody can be great. . . because anybody can serve. You don't have to have a college degree to serve. You don't have to make your subject and verb agree to serve. . . . You only need a heart full of grace. A soul generated by love.

—Martin Luther King, Jr.

A leader learns to give credit for building successes. No matter how small, look for opportunities to praise others for success of the school. Praise your employees to your superiors, parents, students, and community. Write a quick note or e-mail, or place a note of praise in your weekly bulletin. Give credit to others about their performances, especially behind their back. The word will get around that you were praising them. Introducing employees to new people is a perfect situation to praise and give them credit for a success. For example, "This is Mrs. Bagby. She is an outstanding teacher. She and our language arts department recently created a new professional development strategy that is being used in our district. It's unbelievable!" Being a credit maker encourages employees to keep the great ideas coming because they know they will get the lion's share of the praise. Leaders who take credit for the team successes or others' ideas will create a negative environment where sharing or participating ceases. A favorite statement of a principal should be, "I have a bunch of brilliant people who make me look good."

File Ideas

Knowledge is power.

—Francis Bacon

The more you know, the less you need.

—Australian Aboriginal saying

Create a filing system for ideas. You never know when you can use a brilliant idea. Keep copies of speeches, PowerPoint presentations, quotations, and stories on your computer. Ask others for a copy when you see an outstanding idea, policy, or program. Learn to steal and share ideas. You might have to change borrowed ideas to apply them to your school. Be sure to let the people responsible know how you applied their idea in your school. It will make them feel good that they were able to help you. If you make successful changes, then let them know. Learn to give and take on ideas. It can create a continuous sharing of ideas between you and another professional. Cut out newspaper clippings and store in different folders. Create binders for different topics. These sources will be ready when you need them. Learn to occasionally review those saved ideas once or twice a year.

Use E-mail

We struggle with the complexities and avoid the simplicities.

—Norman Vincent Peale

Lost time is never found again.

—John H. Aughey

Use e-mail to help save time and costs. A principal can write a quick note and send it much faster than waiting for the secretary to type the message, copy additional copies, and pass it out to staff. Emails to staff can be forwarded from the superintendent, state education department, or other pertinent sources. Encourage staff to use e-mail. There is not enough time in the day. This is one way to save time for the principal and staff. Paper costs are another consideration. E-mail will decrease your school costs by saving paper.

Praise Twice

The sweetest of all sounds is praise.

—Xenophon

A favorite technique is to praise teacher A when visiting teacher B. Praise their performances, and if possible, relate them somehow to other teachers' successes. There are two motives to praising both a teacher's performance and another teacher's performance. First, the principal should look for something positive witnessed during their visit. Second, teacher B will share any positive praise about teacher A when they get the opportunity.

For example, the principal might share, "Mrs. Schuler, your classroom management is excellent. I don't know if the students were so engaged in your lesson that they don't look for opportunities to misbehave, or if you spent an enormous amount on classroom procedures, or if you have developed positive relationships with the students. It's probably all three. The way your class is structured is similar to Mrs. Goldenberg and Mr. Shourd's classes. The students are always on task and engaged. Our school and students are fortunate to have teachers like you, Mrs. Goldenberg, and Mr. Shourd."

Everyone likes to hear praise. This technique allows each person to be praised twice, once by the principal and a second time by a colleague at a later time. This also reinforces the continuation of positive staff behavior.

Base Decisions on What's Best for the Entire School

The ultimate measure of a man is not where he stands in moments of comfort and convenience, but where he stands at times of challenge and controversy.

—Martin Luther King Jr.

Be careful when making a decision that benefits only a small percentage of people. Leaders will be faced with a decision that could be good for one person. Consider how the decision affects the entire organization. Ask two questions: "What's best for kids or this employee? What's best for the entire school?" A leader does not want to make polices, rules, or decisions for one person if there will be a detrimental effect on the entire school. Make decisions based on what's best for kids but also based on what's best for the entire school. For example, a common gut-wrenching decision for a principal is to suspend a student from school. Let's say a student commits an act that calls for a suspension. We know that it's best for the student to be at school. The student does not need to be at home, doing community service, or running the streets. The student needs to be in class learning. At the same time, it would be best for the rest of the class if the student was suspended. The student is disrupting the learning environment for the rest of the class. Schools have to be safe and provide a positive learning environment. Students should feel safe at school. Principals must keep order, and students should be expected to follow rules. What is best for all the students in this example? The offending student needs to be class, but the rest of the class has a right to come to school and learn. The principal may have to suspend the student because it's best for the entire school.

Avoid Conflicts

Pick battles big enough to matter, small enough to win.

—Jonathan Kozol

Learn to say no with tact. Try to finish every encounter on pleasant terms. A statement when you are confronted with a highly upset person can be, "I'm sorry that you feel this way. It doesn't make me feel good that we disagree. What we do in education is too important for us to have a confrontation. I don't want confrontations with anyone. I try to avoid upsetting a person. It bothers me. I got into education to help others, not upset you and others. I'm sorry that I cannot grant your request." The person might still be upset, but you are sending a message that speaks from the heart that you don't like to say no, but you have to sometimes. Letting people know that you care about their feelings can help them leave with a better feeling toward you.

Some people will be confrontational and in search of a fight. These people cannot be satisfied. A leader won't be able to satisfy their demands, so don't engage in an argument with them. For example, if parents don't want their child to read a selected reading from an approved state and corporation list, gently let the parent know that the student can read a different book at the same reading level. Also, let the parents know that their child has the option to read a different, but approved book when the class engages in discussions on the teacher's chosen book. Giving options will diffuse the situation.

Sometimes the principal will not be able to give alternatives and will have to say no. Learn to diffuse the situations by not arguing. You won't win. A final thought is to avoid engaging in too many wars at one time. Consider the great battles of history. Many leaders lost the war as a consequence of battling on too many fronts. Take heed not to take on too many battles at any one time. It can damage the good works you have accomplished. Doubt will start to emerge from the public if you are engaged in too many battles at one time. A principal does not want to get the reputation of being confrontational. Jerry Patterson (2000) says that leaders who have too many conflicts are like people who have too many rocks in their pockets. *Rocks in pockets* can weight a leader down. One rock is acceptable, a few rocks are tolerable, but too many rocks will sink you. Learn to choose your battles wisely.

Learn to Compromise

Accept good advice gracefully—as long as it doesn't interfere with what you intended to do in the first place.

—Gene Brown

Consider how hard it is to change yourself and you'll understand what little chance you have of trying to change others.

—Jacob M. Braude

Leaders are going to be faced with decisions that they can compromise on. People have to ask themselves if allowing a compromise makes a difference in a given situation. If the answer is no, then compromise; if yes, then consider what you can lose by saying no as compared with a yes answer. For example, in most districts principals will have to make hiring decisions. Say two candidates are equal in ability, experience, enthusiasm, leadership potential, and being positive role models, and your hiring committee favors one candidate over the other. You might think, "Does it matter whom I hire in this case? Both candidates are equal. No, it doesn't matter. I will be extremely pleased with either candidate. Our staff will be pleased with either candidate. Our students will be truly blessed to have either candidate." In this example, you could compromise and agree with the hiring committee on the selection of candidate because the decision doesn't matter in this case. Both candidates are outstanding and equal in every way. Giving in on a decision this time could help you the next time you have to make a decision with this group.

Leaders need to consider the pros and cons of each decision. Occasionally, compromising with a group's demands will be the best decision. Compromising does not make one a coward. The leader needs to consider, "Is it a big deal to compromise on this decision?" "What can I gain from compromising on this request?" "What can I lose by denying this demand?" "How will my decision affect other groups in my building?" "Will my decision have a negative affect on any school policies or rules?" If compromising is not a big deal, then compromise. It doesn't mean giving in if the decision does make a difference. Using the same example, if two candidates are not equal, then the principal has to hire the best regardless of any pressures. If your decision matters, then make your decision based on what's best for your school.

Be Fair

Whenever you are to do a thing, though it can never be known but to yourself, ask yourself how you would act were all the world looking at you, and act accordingly.

—Thomas Jefferson

Treat students and employees fairly when administering consequences. Make sure that students are aware of expectations and consequences. A common act of injustice is to withhold a reward on the day of the event. For example, the principal or teacher decides that a particular student will not attend a field trip on the day of the trip. Nothing was said until the day of the trip, and now it's communicated that a student doesn't deserve to go. That's not fair. Although the student may not deserve to go, it's not fair to wait until the last minute to spring a surprise on a student. What's fair is communicating expectations and consequences when announcing the field trip. Follow this with letting the students and parents know immediately if students' behavior will prevent them from going on the field trip. Don't wait until the last minute to give the "aha" or the "gotcha." Some might get satisfaction, but it's not fair. Likewise, let employees know if actions are inappropriate. It's not fair to wait until evaluation day to discuss those actions. Let people know as soon as possible if behaviors are inappropriate, and tell them what you expect.

Deal Is a Deal

If life deals you lemons then make lemonade.

—Anonymous

There is always time to make right what is wrong.

—Susan Griffin

Sometimes a leader will make a bad decision. Only change decisions when it will benefit a student or employee. For example, if a student was suspended for one day when a three-day suspension was justified, don't change the decision and make it a three-day suspension. However, if a student is given a three-day suspension, but a one-day suspension was justified, by all means change it to benefit the student. Learn to err on the side of the student or employee. Once you make a decision, don't change it unless it benefits the person. A deal is a deal. Move on, learn from it, but don't go back on your decision and give a harsher punishment.

Agree to Disagree

We should ever conduct ourselves towards our enemy as if he were one day to be our friend.

—John Henry Newman

Peace and harmony between people is paramount to a healthy school environment. Students will have occasional conflicts with students, and employees will have occasional disagreements with other employees. For example, if two employees are in disagreement, the principal should encourage the two people to meet alone and discuss the situation. If an accord cannot be reached, the principal may have to intervene and meet with both people. Meeting privately before coming together is good advice. It allows each individual to air his or her honest feelings. This allows the principal to gain an understanding of the situation. Meet with both people, encouraging them to work out their differences while guiding their conversation. The last resort is for the principal to dictate rules for the future if the two people cannot come to an agreement. Guidelines include the following: Each person agrees not to speak negatively about the other individual; each person agrees to treat each other respectfully; and each person agrees not to believe rumors or gossip from a third person (because both people agreed to treat each other respectfully and not talk negatively about each other). The principal may have to have each person repeat each rule in the meeting. It might seem childish, but it helps reinforce the agreement.

Spend Time Focused on Staff

A single day is enough to make us a little larger.

—Paul Klee

Leaders need to make time to think about their entire staff on a regular basis. Reflect and ask, "What am I doing well? What could I be doing differently? Am I doing anything that is inhibiting their efforts? What do I need to stop doing immediately? What do I need to start doing immediately? Have I supported staff efforts to succeed? Have I given everyone opportunities to lead in our building? Am I including everyone in the decision-making process? Is every employee giving his or her personal best? What could I do to ensure that every employee is giving their best effort?" Research conducted found significant differences with principals spending more time focused on their less effective teachers than on their more effective teachers (Fleck, 2003). When principals are asked about how much time they should devote to instructional leadership, "they invariably answer, more than they actually are" (Glatthorn, 1998). Servgiovanni (2001) has cited a study showing that principals spend much less time on the job engaged in instructional activities than they feel that they should. The subjects in this study said that they spent much more time than they would prefer on (1) budget, administration, and maintenance; (2) parent engagement and relations; and (3) student contact and discipline. Similarly, teachers said that classroom observations by the principal were infrequent "and largely symbolic" (Johnson, 1990). The National Forum on Educational Leadership (1999) recently reaffirmed that the most important task of principals is to provide instructional leadership. The No Child Left Behind Act calls for a continuous school improvement plan. This should be a major focus for every building principal, but the reality is that it is not. Research has shown that principals are spending more time on noninstructional activities such as (1) regularly checking lesson plans, (2) approving parent correspondence, (3) closely following contract obligations, (4) ensuring that assigned lesson plans are being used for instructional or school duties, and (5) documenting the negative actions of their less effective teachers. Principals need to focus on instructional leadership, staff development, and student achievement. All employees from struggling to great need a leader's time. Spend time reflecting on all employees and what they need to succeed.

Schedule Regular Classroom Visits

I was taught the way of progress is neither swift nor easy.

—Marie Curie

Plan regular classroom observations. Write visits into your schedule. Principals are more likely to make visits if they are planned into the weekly schedule. Make it a habit. The most important thing in schools is what is happening in the classrooms. Student achievement and student improvement is what it's all about. How can principals understand and improve student achievement if they are not consistently in classrooms? All teachers need to be visited by the principal. A common habit is to visit teachers who need assistance more often. There are significant differences in the amount of time that principals spend in the classrooms of the less effective teachers versus time spent in the more effective teachers' classrooms (Fleck, 2003). This leads to the conclusion that principals spend more time observing less effective teaching methods than outstanding teaching methods. If principals are going to help their less effective teachers, principals should observe the innovative, effective instruction methods of their more effective teachers. The same research found principals limiting visits to their more effective teachers, but they were able to identify and use these same teachers to mentor others and train university students. One reason cited on limiting classroom visits was to give more classroom autonomy to more effective teachers. Higher teacher ratings of principals were associated with the provision of supportive feedback that was specific and detailed, based on actual classroom observation, and expressed in a nonjudgmental manner with the availability of follow-up sessions (Blasé & Blasé, 1999). Principals spend less time in the more effective classrooms, but improvement is needed for all teachers. Visiting and providing feedback to a school's more effective teachers is critical because, in their teacher-leadership roles, these same teachers can help others.

Suggest Ideas to Staff

Leadership is the art of getting someone else to do something you want done because he wants to do it.

—Dwight D. Eisenhower

Learn to avoid issuing orders to employees. Instead, suggest or imply ideas. Maintaining a balance between issuing orders and offering counsel can be tough. Create an atmosphere where the employee might think it's their idea. The success of the plan has a greater rate of success if ownership is created in the employee. Issuing an order may cause the employee to resist it. A favorite method is to talk about someone the employee respects and a successful idea that person used at school.

The principal doesn't suggest that they adopt the technique. The principal mentions it in a bragging sort of way and drops it. Hopefully, the employee will think about it, maybe adopt it, or even adopt a part of the idea. Make sure that the employee respects the person you mention. If the employee does not respect the person you mention, then they most likely will oppose the idea. For example, the principal could say, "Have you heard about Mr. Eade's 10th-grade language arts class? He wrote and was awarded a grant from the Rotary Club. High school students read to all first graders in the district. It's a great idea that focused on the standards and collaboration of the students in our school district. I'm not sure who enjoyed it more, the high school students or the first graders. We received several positive comments from elementary teachers, students, parents, and the press."

The principal's purpose could be for the teachers to write grants. Another purpose could be to develop collaborative activities with the elementary or middle school students. A third possibility could be to think out of the box and create engaging lessons that focus on the academic standards. Hopefully, teachers will think about your comments and plan a future activity in their respected areas. A second possibility is to have meetings in a teacher's classroom. It allows the opportunity to engage in conversation about the setup of the room, materials on the walls, programs, and great things occurring in the classroom. A third possibility is to have faculty meetings at different schools. Visiting other schools provides the opportunity to see what others are doing in the district. It's a great way to suggest ideas to staff without saying a word.

Know When to Help

The best executive is the one who has sense enough to pick good men to do what he wants done, and self-restraint enough to keep from meddling with them while they do it.

—Theodore Roosevelt

First Who . . . Then What

—Jim Collins

When faced with a decision, leaders look at each opportunity, consider employees' talents, consider concerns, and match an employee's talent with the opportunity. A leader should share a vision of success, guidelines, and possible pitfalls to avoid. The leader's main job is to offer support to the employee in charge of each task after outlining a vision. A leader will learn to do less when staff needs less help and do more when staff needs more help. Some employees will need a leader's coaching, while others will need the leader to get out of their way. Leaders should have regular updates by the team leaders, no matter their strength.

Check Lesson Plans

Good teaching is one-fourth preparation and three-fourths theater.

—Gail Godwin

Krug wrote, "Effective leaders provide information that teachers need to plan their classes effectively and they actively support curriculum development" (Krug, 1992). A principal should regularly check lesson plans. The leader should require teachers to leave plans on their desks. Let staff members know that you will review lessons, and ask them to leave lessons in an assigned place so you may look at your leisure when the teachers have gone home. This allows you the flexibility to check plans in mornings, evenings, or weekends. Another possibility is to check lessons on a regular and flexible schedule. For example, the principal may check the lessons in language arts one week, followed by the math lessons the next week. Research has supported that principals need to closely supervise teachers, intervening directly to upgrade their competencies and to correct any shortcomings in their classroom practices (Beck & Murphy, 1993; Bossert, 1996). Research conducted found principals spending more time checking the lesson plans of less effective teachers than their more effective teachers (Fleck, 2003). If staff members know that the principal will check lessons, they will be encouraged to plan appropriately each week. Checking lessons will also encourage teachers to be prepared in the event that they are absent, and a substitute teacher is placed in their classroom. It is embarrassing and frustrating to try to figure out what a substitute should do if the regular teacher does not have lesson plans. A class with no lessons usually becomes a wasted day of worksheets, videotapes, or survival to keep the students engaged.

Train Your Employees

Give a man a fish and he will eat for a day. Teach a man to fish and he will eat for the rest of his life.
—Chinese Proverb

Small opportunities are often the beginning of great enterprises.
—Demosthenes

School improvement and staff improvement are important if schools are to increase student achievement. Keep professional development as a top priority in your school. Have staff set professional development goals and monitor their efforts. Ensure that employees collaborate and develop the school improvement plan. A continuous school improvement plan should include professional development plans for the entire staff. It is important that every employee participate in staff development. Training every employee helps to create ownership as you follow the school improvement plan. Second, every employee will have a common language to share after professional development sessions. Third, it helps with team building when every person is involved in training.

Unfortunately, money is becoming scarce, and professional development is usually one of the first programs cut during financial hardships, even though most experts agree that it's one of the most important aspects of successful schools. Leaders have to invest in their employees. If no money is available for professional development, use the Internet, borrow books, share with other schools, but train your employees. A principal sometimes has to be creative in providing professional development for staff. A possibility is to give employees time during the day to share with colleagues. For example, the principal may bring in visitors to read, speak, or provide demonstrations for the students. Scheduling university professors, businesses, or community agencies to talk with the students on age-appropriate topics is another possibility. The principal could supervise the students while staff is involved in professional development. Leaders need to build an environment where every staff person has the opportunity to learn and grow. This can be accomplished through reading, workshops, discussion groups, the Internet, and faculty discussions. Motivated staff will usually pursue these opportunities. A leader must be on the lookout and create an environment for all staff to learn and grow. Leaders will ensure opportunities for the obvious employees, but think about learning and growth opportunities for low performers, secretaries, paraprofessionals, health professionals, custodians, bus drivers, and cafeteria staff.

Limit Classroom Interruptions

The quality of an individual is reflected in the standards they set for themselves.

—Ray Kroc

Avoid interrupting classes with too many disruptions. Schedule a time every day for announcements. Some schools have morning announcements, whereas others have afternoon announcements. The principals need to preserve instructional and learning time. If a parent drops off a project, glasses, money, or some item, then have an office worker deliver the item. Avoid calling the student from class to the office or having the parent deliver the item to the student. It's a good excuse for the principal to get out of the office and visit the classroom while delivering the item. There is only so much time in the school day and not enough time to cover the academic standards. The principal needs to be conscious of interruptions and make adjustments to limit them. Avoid making announcements calling for the custodian or principal. A leader needs to demand that the intercom be used for emergencies only. I told my secretary not to use the intercom for me unless someone was dying or an out-of-control person was in the building. School board members or superintendents who call can wait until I get back to my office. Visiting classrooms with staff and students is more important than an intercom interruption to answer a telephone call from my superiors. It becomes too easy to use the intercom during the day. Invest in radios for the custodians and principals. I suggest that you chart how many times the intercom is used and work toward decreasing the use of it. Monitor the use of the intercom so it does not detract from the learning environment and take away from instruction.

Don't Limit Visits to Allow Classroom Autonomy

If you have a talent, use it in every which way possible. Don't hoard it. Don't dole it out like a miser. Spend it lavishly like a millionaire intent on going broke.

—Brendan Francis

The leader needs to be aware that visiting great teachers' classrooms is important, too. Principals must see the great works of the building to share with others. Too often principals visit only poor teachers' classrooms. Research supports that principals restrict classroom visits to their more effective teachers to allow more classroom autonomy than they do with their less effective teachers (Fleck, 2003). If the principal only saw poor teachers at work, it could lower a principal's standard of appropriate and quality teaching. Principals need to witness outstanding teachers working with students and see students engaged in high-quality student work. Classroom excellence and innovative teaching strategies must be observed and shared with the entire school community. Get in the habit of visiting all classrooms to share the great things happening in your school.

Send Cards to Staff

Treat people as if they were what they ought to be and you help them to become what they are capable of being.

— Johann Wolfgang Von Goethe

A good deed is never lost; he who sows courtesy reaps friendship, and he who plants kindness gathers love.

— Saint Basil

Send thank-you notes, birthday cards, sympathy cards, get well cards, congratulatory cards, and so forth to your staff. They will appreciate your thoughtfulness. It creates a warm feeling and sense of belonging.

Remember students', staff members', and friends' birthdays. A quick e-mail or phone call to a friend, boss, or coworker will bring joy to each. Announcing birthdays during morning messages or placing birthday announcements in your newsletters is another method. Remembering birthdays is a small way to make others feel good that you remember them.

Include Staff in Evaluation Process

Real education consists in drawing the best out of yourself.

—Mohandas K. Gandhi

True education is to learn how to think, not what to think.

—Krishnamurti

Make staff evaluations a mutual process with employees for professional development. Have them develop specific goals that include short- and long-term goals. Employees who develop ownership in the process are more likely to work toward the established goals. Let them make recommendations for areas of improvement. Let employees know that you want them to develop a few goals each year. It helps to include them in the process. During the evaluation, ask employees the following questions: What went well for you this year? What didn't start well but finished well? What are some areas for improvement? What can I as an administrator do to help you be more successful? If there was anything you could change, what would it be? What would you like to do differently next year?

Be an Instructional Leader

Great teachers are made one student at a time.

—Todd Whitaker

Become an expert on curriculum and instruction. Learn best practices and preferred teaching methods. Encourage your staff to become experts of the academic standards. Make it a practice that teachers incorporate the academic standards into their daily lessons. Engage in daily conversations that focus on the academic standards. Routinely ask students, "What did you learn today or what are you learning today? Principals, teachers, and students who regularly engage in dialogue will begin to know the academic standards without referencing sources. The National Association of Secondary School Principals (2002) position is that the role of principal is to promote excellence in school leadership. According to the NASSP, the instructional leader of the school promotes the success of all students by facilitating the development, articulation, implementation, and stewardship of a vision of learning that the principal develops in cooperation with the school community. The principal strives to make schools a positive learning environment by setting high expectations for each student and teacher. The principal is also the manager of the school, responsible for the legal, fiscal, and operational functions that provide an infrastructure for learning. Effective principals combine both instructional and managerial roles to foster student success and teacher effectiveness. In regard to school improvement, principals must ensure the culture of continuous improvement in their schools in terms of school climate, instructional programs, and instructional facilities. The National Association of Elementary School Principals (2004) outlined six standards: Effective principals lead schools in a way that places students and adult learning at the center. Effective principals set high expectations and standards for the academic and social development of all students and the performance of adults. Effective principals demand content and instruction that ensure student achievement of agreed upon academic standards. Effective principals create a culture of continuous learning for adults tied to student learning and other school goals. Effective principals use multiple sources of data as diagnostic tools to assess, identify, and apply instructional improvement. Effective principals actively engage the community to create shared responsibility for student and school success. School leaders must learn to become more than a manager if students are to improve.

Focus on
Student Engagement

Inspiration and imagination go hand in hand.

—Anonymous

Principals need to pay more attention to the actions of the students when visiting classrooms. Too many lessons are designed with the teacher's performance in mind. We want teachers to be the guide on the side as compared to being the sage on the stage. Consider whether the students are engaged in meaningful tasks or is the teacher the primary focus of the lesson. Who is working harder, the student or the teacher? Schlechty (2002) says that real student improvement can occur only as authentic student engagement increases. Schlechty's framework of Working on the Work presents ten qualities that teachers can use to make student tasks more meaningful: (1) *Content and substance:* refers to what is to be learned and the level of student interest in the subject or topic. (2) *Organization of knowledge:* work is organized, as well as the learning styles that are assumed or are to be addressed. (3) *Product focus:* structuring tasks and activities to be learned to some product, performance, or exhibition to which the student attaches personal value. (4) *Clear and compelling product standards:* students are clear about what they are to do, what the products they produce should look like, what standards will be applied to evaluate these products and their performances. (5) *Protection from adverse consequences for initial failures:* tasks are designed so students feel free to try without fear for initial failures. (6) *Affirmation of performance:* designing tasks and activities so that the performance of students is made visible to persons who are significant in their lives whose opinions the student values and cares about. (7) *Affiliation:* designing tasks so that students are provided the opportunity to work with peers, parents, or others. (8) *Choice:* designing tasks and activities so that students can exercise choice either in what they are to learn or how the go about learning that which it is required that they learn. (9) *Novelty and variety:* providing students the opportunity to employ a wide range of media and approaches when engaged in the activities assigned. (10) *Authenticity:* linking learning tasks to things that are of real interest to students. It is not assumed that every lesson has these ten attributes but it is a list of possibilities when planning student tasks for a lesson.

Be a Nurturing Leader

The ultimate responsibility of a leader is to facilitate other people's development as well as his own.

—Fred Pryor

I praise loudly, I blame softly.

—Catherine the Great

Educators are in the people business. Helping others and being nurturing is what educators do best. Principals set the tone. Be a leader who shows compassion toward all staff and students. Cash (1997) reported that good leaders set a positive tone and give the gifts of love and significance. Fleck (2003) reported differences between how principals let their more effective teachers know that they care about them as people and how they approached their less-effective staff. Some school leaders think that they will be taken advantage of if they show compassion and take an active interest in the personal lives of employees and students. Principals can be compassionate and lead at the same time. School leaders do not have to have a stone heart to have control and respect. Be a caring leader, a nurturing leader, a helping leader, a compassionate leader, a humanistic leader, a people-person leader, and a loving leader. Principals must model these behaviors with staff and students if their school's climate is going to be positive.

Recognize Staff Accomplishments

People look at you and me to see what they are supposed to be. And, if we don't disappoint them, maybe, they won't disappoint us.

—Walt Disney

Leaders should catch their staff doing things well. Focus on the positives, not the negatives. Recognize successes. Recognize staff accomplishments. Look daily for ways to recognize, encourage, and show appreciation for staff efforts. Be a leader who is looking for staff doing good things rather than always looking for bad things. An employee once submitted an anonymous complaint to our faculty cabinet. Our cabinet meets every month to address staff concerns. The complaint stated that another employee would occasionally forget to show up for assigned duty. All employees were assigned a morning and afternoon duty every four weeks. My statement to the cabinet was, I can do one of four things. I can address the entire faculty to stress the importance of showing up for assigned duties, but who wants to listen to me complain about something they didn't do? If it was me, I would think: Talk to the guilty person, not all of us. Second, you can let me know who the guilty person is, and I will address it with that person, but I assume that you don't want to tell me the person's name. I respect that. The third option is for you to politely and privately let the guilty person know. The fourth option is for me to sneak around and try to catch who is not showing up for duty. I don't know if it's morning duty, afternoon duty, or lunch supervision. I got into education to catch people doing good things, not sneak around catching people making mistakes. I concluded with, "What would you recommend, because I can do any of the four? Do you want me to speak to you and the rest of the faculty for something you didn't do? Do you want me to sneak around and catch you doing something wrong? What do you suggest?" My faculty cabinet wisely decided that one of them would talk to the guilty person, and if the situation didn't improve, they would let me know the guilty person's name.

A principal has to be in the habit of recognizing successes and catching people doing great things. Use as many opportunities as possible to compliment others. Get in the habit of saying something positive about the person or their abilities every time you come in contact with them.

Use Tact
When Reprimanding Staff

Honest criticism is hard to take, particularly from a relative, a friend, an acquaintance, or a stranger.

—Franklin P. Jones

Your job gives you authority. Your behavior earns you respect.

—Irwin Federman

Have a private conversation when dealing with a personal or negative topic. Always allow people the opportunity to save their dignity by being addressed alone. Very few enjoy being singled out in public especially in front of their peers or students. Give employees the same respect that you would appreciate, and make all sensitive conversations private if possible. Leaders learn to use tact when correcting or even reprimanding an employee. Keep in mind that you don't want to totally destroy an employee to the point that the person will be incapable of contributing in the school setting. A leader wants behavior change. Leaders occasionally have to correct employees, but use caution that you don't instill hatred in the employee. Allow employees to save their dignity when correcting them. Correct in private and in a caring manner. Let the employees know that you care about them. Let the employees know that their behavior is uncharacteristic, and you are confident that they will not let it happen again. Fully outline what behaviors you expect. Give suggestions to the employees along with any support to help them. An employee destroyed is lost forever.

Document
Negative Actions of Staff

Good teachers cost a lot, but poor teachers cost a lot more.

—Anonymous

Leaders should have frequent conversations on expectations. Give guidance and support in both formal and informal conversations. Inappropriate behaviors should not be ignored. A principal needs to do everything possible before documenting negative employee actions, but at some point in time, it has to happen. Formally writing a person up is the last step an administrator wants to take, but it might be the only way to get an employee to exhibit desired behaviors or eliminate inappropriate behaviors. A leader wants behavior change. People are different, and the leader has to figure out the best method to change an employee's behavior. Talking will work with some, whereas documenting is the only way for others. Research found significant differences with principals in documenting the negative actions of their less effective teachers as compared with their more effective teachers (Fleck, 2003). It is not surprising that principals tolerated the mistakes of their more effective teachers and documented the negative actions of their less effective teachers. Research concludes that principals were more tolerant of mistakes to a point, but they would document the negative actions of less effective teachers. I also surmise that principals can only discuss appropriate behavior or expectations for so long. It appears that effective teachers would make the necessary changes and/or not repeat the inappropriate behaviors. The repeat offenders—defiant and incompetent teachers—were having their actions documented by principals.

Contracts with Staff

Always design a thing by considering it in its next larger context, a chair in a room, a room in a house, a house in an environment, an environment in a city plan.

—Eliel Saarinen

Dufour (1999) shared that principals lead through shared vision and collective commitments rather than through rules and authority. Contracts are important, but results are more important. Don't become too obsessed with enforcing every policy and rule. If teachers, staff, and principals followed the contract to the letter, we might not get anything done as well as when we allow a few rules to be occasionally waived. For example, letting employees leave a few minutes early on an occasional Friday after an evening program the night before helps to build a positive relationship with staff. It sends a message to employees that you appreciated their participation the night before and will let them leave after the students are gone for the day. Most employees are giving above and beyond what the contract states. Principals need to be aware and occasionally reciprocate in return.

However, a principal may have some staff not performing at an acceptable level. Research found that principals followed contract obligations with their less effective teachers more often than with their more effective teachers (Fleck, 2003). Many mediocre employees want to get the same allowances as (or more than) the rest of the staff. For example, it doesn't bother me when an outstanding teacher is a few minutes late one day. Great teachers spend an enormous amount of time giving beyond the scheduled workday. They usually lead school committees, arrive early, stay late, and volunteer to help the principal, students, parents, and school. Mediocre teachers will expect the principal to allow them always to be late and leave early. In fact, they will usually point out that you allowed the great teacher to come in late four months ago and didn't say anything. A principal needs to be aware that poor employees are always looking when you don't enforce a rule. They want the occasional to be the norm. I ask if they really want to compare themselves to the great teacher. I will further list everything that the outstanding teacher does for students, parents, and the school. The conversation is usually over as I state again that I don't think they really want to compare themselves to the outstanding teacher.

Make Students
Give Written Statements

In the arsenal of truth, there is no greater weapon than fact.

—Lyndon B. Johnson

When investigating a situation, first, have students give written statements. You may have to take notes for younger students. A common student habit is to use *they, he,* and *she* instead of names. Insist that students write full names in the statement, so there is no misunderstanding about who did what. Second, instruct students to only write facts that they personally witnessed. Another common student habit is to tell details that someone else told them. Many students believe these details to be facts. Next, read their papers to clear up any misunderstandings. Ask if anything has been left out. Tell them, "I don't want any surprises." Ask the students if they understand what you mean by no surprises. Explain that you don't want any details left out before talking to other individuals.

A common student habit is to say that they didn't do anything. For example, let's say a student is in your office letting you know that a student started a fight with him or her. Make sure students don't leave out important details, such as that they hit back. It may help you determine the credibility of the student's story. This is what is meant by "no surprises." Having students write the facts is crucial, in the event that any students try to change their story. It's too easy to change verbal statements. Next, compare the written documents and ask questions. Take notes as the students tell you the facts. Note taking helps to catch discrepancies between verbal statements and written statements.

Always bring the main people together at the conclusion to recap their stories. Give each student an opportunity to state the facts. Do not let students interrupt when another student is speaking. Let the student know that he or she will get an opportunity to give their side of the story. You may have to ask questions to clear up discrepancies if the people have different stories. The last step is to go back to each person to ask if anything is missing or is there anything he or she wants to add. Ask, "Is there anything missing? Is there anything more that you want to add? Are you leaving anything out?" This is important in case the student tells a parent a different story. A principal wants to let the parent know that they had an opportunity to give their side of the story.

Encourage Honesty

Right is more precious than peace.

—Woodrow Wilson

When investigating a situation, always let students know that you appreciate people who are honest. You want to plant a seed in their subconscious that honesty is more important than the accused action. You could ask, "If you are being honest, then I have no problems, but if I find out you are not being honest or you are leaving out details, then I'm going to be upset. I don't mind if people make mistakes. I would rather someone say 'I did it,' and be done with it. I appreciate honesty, but if you make me spend an enormous amount of time investigating this to find the truth, then I'm going to be ticked off. So are you telling me everything? Is this the story you want to stick to?" If the student sticks to the story, my response will be, "Fair enough." Many students will stick to their stories, but some would rather take a perceived lighter punishment than taking an unknown harsher punishment. Make it a point to commend students who admit when they are at fault. A principal wants to acknowledge a student's honesty. Students who are honest will save you an enormous amount of time. You can spend hours investigating a situation trying to find the truth. You may say, "I like people who don't try to weasel their way out of mistakes. I'm still going to do what I need to do, but I do appreciate honesty. No one is perfect. We all make mistakes, but we don't have to make two mistakes by lying." I use the word *weasel* because I want to psychologically challenge them. Students do not want to be known as weak and sneaky. I also use an offensive word like *lying* because they are being honest. It helps them to think about being honest this time and any time in the future.

When you call parents, make sure to praise their child first before you tell them what happened. It helps to soften the blow. For example, you may begin, "I want to let you know that your child was honest with me. I appreciate people who don't try to weasel out on me and who are honest. I'm still going to do what I need to do, but I do appreciate honesty." Before asking what happened, parents will usually confide that they work hard on instilling honesty in their child. Likewise, end the conversation by bragging about their child's honesty. The next time this same student is in your office, brag about how honest they were the time before. Do this because you want the student to be honest this time, too. It helps to reinforce the behavior to be honest and truthful.

Is This the
First Time You Have Done This?

You can tell whether a man is clever by his answers. You can tell whether a man is wise by his questions.

—Naguib Mahfouz

Some students will not be honest about their involvement in a negative behavior. Let's say that you have a high probability of suspicion that a student did something, but she will not admit to doing it. You may even have witnesses who say the accused did it. In the heat of the moment, I like to ask, "Is this the first time that you have done this?" This question causes confusion. Commonly, the student answers yes followed by dropping her head, knowing that she has finally been honest with me. A student would rather be accused of doing something only once. I usually don't care because I am seeking the truth today. Students don't want me to think that they have done this before. A common answer is, "No. . . yes. . . no. . . yes." Use this question when emotions are high. It helps to ensure the success of student confusion—which means the student is thinking about his or her behavior.

Use Peer Pressure

People only see what they are prepared to see.

—Ralph Waldo Emerson

Peer pressure can help with honesty when investigating a student concern. If you suspect a student is being dishonest, then have him repeat his side of the story in front of everyone involved. You are playing on his relationships with the other students. This confrontational technique is more successful if some of the students are friends.

Many students would rather admit their mistakes than damage a relationship. Bring students together and have each student repeat to you and the group what he or she did. Each student gets a turn to confess his or her mistake. Leave the nonconfessing student until last in the hope that he will confess after the others have set the momentum. If the student still doesn't confess, the other students will usually give a look of disbelief and start berating him for not being honest. The peer pressure will usually force the one student to admit his actions. If the student doesn't come clean, he will get a far greater punishment when he leaves your office. The student in question knows this and will probably admit his part.

A second technique is to have the student wait outside your office as you talk privately with a witness. If the witness does not give any information, walk her out and send her back to class very quickly. Do not allow the student waiting outside your office to talk to her, but let them see one another. The student who was waiting did not know what the other student told me. I would tell the student when I talked to him that I had been told some disturbing news and ask if there is there anything he wished to tell me. I would play on the hunch that the student would be honest with me because he suspected that the previous student had told me the truth.

Another variation on this technique is to leave the student in your office as you talk to witnesses. Mention that you are going to talk to some students as you leave the student to ponder the situation. If the witnesses do not give any useful information, you may say to the student in your office that you have been talking to several witnesses and are disturbed by what they told you. Again give the perception that witnesses gave conflicting stories. If the student sticks to the story, you may give a look of confusion. You have not said what the witnesses said, but act as though they gave a different account of what transpired.

Call Home Before the Student Gets Home

It takes time to save time.

—Joe Taylor

If an incident occurs, make sure that you are the first to inform the parents. If a student has participated in inappropriate behavior, after thoroughly investigating the situation, including taking student statements, call the parents from your office with the student present. . This gives the student the opportunity to dispel any misinformation and helps to decrease the chance that the student will change her story. If the student changes the facts later, and the parents call you, reply, "I'm confused. Your child was present when I explained the situation to you. She gave me statements before I called you. She gave me a written statement. She had ample opportunity to correct any erroneous statements. It's strange that she waited until she got home to finally remember the real story." Some students will change the facts regardless of the situation. Some students learn to cause doubt and redirect inappropriate behavior on others. Some parents will even make the excuse that their child was afraid to tell the truth in your office. This is pure nonsense, but some parents desperately want to believe their children. You might ask the parents, "Your child was not telling the truth because she was afraid? Now you tell me she is telling the truth. How do we know which is the truth? What she said earlier, or now? What would you think if you were in my chair? I'm only human."

A student left to spread the news can change the facts dramatically. If a student gets an injury (no matter how small), make sure to call home before the student gets home. The principal doesn't want a parent to have only their child's side of the story. It's guaranteed that an upset parent will call and put you on the defensive. Principals can save themselves this headache by being the first to call. If another student touches or injures their child, call to let them know what happened and assure them that you will take care of it. If a student is injured, the nurse or another staff member should call and let the parents know about the injury. You might mention that you think their child is OK, but it's their call. Some parents might come to the school; most will stay home; but all will appreciate that you called about the minor injury. The principal never wants an injured or sick student to go home without parent contact.

Conflict Resolution

I hear and I forget. I see and I remember. I do and I understand.

—Confucius

Teach students to settle conflicts. Conflict resolution programs should be considered at any grade level for staff and students alike. Settling differences in a peaceful and acceptable way is a lifelong skill. There is a tendency for adults to settle student conflicts. Resist the temptation to take over too quickly and settle the situation before the students have had an opportunity to work it out for themselves. Don't let a situation escalate into a fight. A principal needs to use good judgment.

I used to supervise open gym with another teacher where our job was to open the gym and let kids run off steam. Once, when students were playing softball, they depended on us to call the batter out or safe. We wanted the students to learn how to settle conflicts themselves, so we began to make calls against the person asking for a judgment call. For example, when a student would look at us and ask if the student was safe or out, we would respond with the opposite call of whomever was asking. If a student was playing field and asked if the runner was safe or out, the opposite call was safe. If a student from the hitting team asked for a call, we would respond that the runner was out. Some calls were ridiculously wrong, and the students soon learned not to ask us because they would not like our decisions. The students learned to settle the conflict themselves. If the situation escalated into an argument, the game was over. The game might be over for days if the argument became too big. The students wanted to play ball, so they learned not to argue, but instead to settle the conflict in a peaceful manner and have fun.

Let Kids Work It Out

By far, the best proof is experience.

—Sir Francis Bacon

A favorite technique for two friends who have a love-hate relationship is to have them work it out. Use this if you feel they won't get into a fight or argument. Instruct the students to sit in a nearby area and tell them, "Don't come back until you both are in agreement on a story." They usually work it out and come to see you within a short time. This technique is fast and doesn't take much of your time. If this becomes a habit, and they are missing class time, however, you may have to come up with a different solution. You may say, "You are right; this is important, and we need to work it out. I want both of you to report to my office during lunch when we can talk it out. This is important, and I want to give you both the time you deserve." Students feel that lunch is their time. Students don't mind missing class time but are reluctant to give up their social time. Insist that the students report to you and eat lunch in the office. The students may catch you later and let you know that they have worked it out, but you should insist that they still report to you. Tell them, "I want to make sure and hear all of the details, so I will see you at lunch." Do this to drive home a point: They are not going to miss class time in the future so they can work it out. If the students seem to enjoy eating together in your office, then you may have to meet before or after school to discuss the situation. This will make the students think twice the next time they wish to work it out in the office, yet encourage them to work out their own problems—a lifelong skill. Another variation on this technique is to leave students alone in your office. Only use this if you feel the situation will not escalate. You may ask, "Will you two be OK if I leave you together?" The plan is to have the students work out the situation themselves. Make up an excuse that you have to take care of some urgent matter as they discuss the situation. Tell the students that they are not to talk while you are gone, knowing full well that you want them to talk it out. Return within 10 minutes to read their body language. If their body language tells you that they are beginning to work it out, leave again for another 10 to 15 minutes. Repeat leaving and returning until the students let you know that they have already worked it out and are OK with each other. You won't have to ask; the students will let you know when they are ready to talk to you. The principal's part is to fully make sure that they are OK with each other. You can ask, "Is there anything I need to do?" You want to make sure everything is OK in case the students have an argument later. Remind the students that they both said everything was OK, and they didn't need you to do anything if they have a future argument.

Conduct Locker Searches

Honest hearts produce honest actions.

—Brigham Young

Occasionally, it will be reported that a student has contraband or an inappropriate item at school. Consider searching a locker unbeknownst to the students while they are in class. Do this for several reasons. First, you want to establish if students have any contraband at school. Second, it allows you to ask questions and check students' honesty. Third, their honesty may have some influence on what action you take.

Let's say you find cigarettes in a coat. Leave the cigarettes in the locker. Of course, you should never leave the item in the locker if it is drugs, a large knife, or a gun. Only use this technique with less dangerous items of contraband.

Next, go to the student's class and escort him to the office. Once in your office, ask, "Do you have anything at school that you should not have?" You know the answer to the question, but it allows the student to be honest. You may give a lighter punishment when the student is honest. If the answer is no, escort the student to the locker and repeat the question, "Do you have anything at school that you should not have?"

The next step is to ask the student to show everything in his locker. Let the student determine which item to pick. A guilty person will usually save the coat for last if that is where the cigarettes are located. Repeat the question after each item the student shows you in hopes that he will be honest. When you finally get to the coat where the item is hidden, typically, a student will try to show an empty pocket while cleverly hiding the item. Repeat the question one last time before you get the cigarettes. Repeating the question over and over helps to establish if the student is being deceptive.

If a student was honest from the beginning, you might be more lenient. For example, a student has a small penknife and confesses early, sharing the information that the weekend was spent with Grandpa on a campout. It's understandable that the student forgot the small knife was in the bag. This could happen. We are more forgiving when people are honest. This line of questioning sometimes helps to determine if a student is being honest or deceptive. This technique will help when having to explain to parents what consequences will occur. It helps to explain each step and how you gave ample opportunities for the student to be honest.

Encourage Staff to Communicate Both Positive and Negative Consequences to Parents

See everything, overlook a great deal, correct a little.

—Pope John XXII

Great teachers routinely call parents with student concerns. Teachers are hesitant to make parent telephone calls when they lack self-confidence, are inferior or lazy teachers, or have made a mistake in judgment. Principals should encourage teachers to make calls on a regular basis, to instill a "no surprises" work ethic. If there is a student concern, then teachers should communicate that concern to parents. Stress to teachers that they do not want a student giving all the details first. Students will sometimes leave out important details or slant the details in their favor.

Another common mistake is to let an interim report or report card be the first communication with a parent that something is amiss. A principal is defenseless against a parent who says, "If only I had known." How can you argue with that statement? The focus of the conversation becomes the lack of communication from the school instead of the student's behavior. Who knows more about that classroom than the teacher? This is a good reason to encourage teachers to make telephone calls. If a teacher is consistently making poor decisions, the teacher will learn to change after a few unpleasant parent phone calls. Great principals and teachers learn to share both positive and negative telephone calls with parents. Parents are more accepting of negative messages when positive messages are routinely communicated. The best educators will make 10 or more positive telephone calls for every negative telephone call, making it easier for a parent to swallow the negative telephone call after having received several positive calls. Regular parent communication helps to build a positive relationship between the school and parents.

Encourage Concerned Parents to Meet with Staff

You cannot shake hands with a clenched fist.

—Indira Gandhi

Our task. . . is not to fix the blame for the past, but to fix the course for the future.

—John F. Kennedy

Too often, parents will bypass the teacher and call the principal or even the central office with a concern. Effective principals learn to have concerned parents talk with the teacher first. Research found that principals encouraged effective teachers to handle the majority of their discipline problems more often than their ineffective teachers (Fleck, 2003). Todd Whitaker (1997) cited that one major difference between effective and less effective principals was the identification and use of effective teachers at the more effective schools. Miller (2001) reported that "until principals can significantly reduce the time they spend on parent concerns and other non instructional management issues imploring them to engage in more instructional leadership will do little."

Encourage your staff to meet with parents who have concerns. You can easily become a go-between for a teacher and a parent, so you should try to eliminate having to run back and forth, gathering information, between the two people. A teacher is the best source of information about what is going on in the classroom. The teachers are the classroom experts, so let them handle parents, allowing you to attend to other concerns. Let each staff member know that the two of you can meet together with parents who may be confrontational. Your role is to offer support with upset parents.

Occasionally, I will encourage parents to meet with a teacher if I feel the teacher is continuously making poor decisions. Let the teacher take the heat. It's too easy to make a mistake and let the principal deal with the parent. Consider letting an upset parent meet with the teacher alone. A teacher will learn to rethink their poor choices if they get chewed out too many times. If the teacher suspects a confrontation and wants you to be present, then make an excuse to leave early in the meeting. Hopefully, the teacher will not want this to happen too often and will make better decisions in the future.

Keep Parents Happy

Profit in business comes from repeat customers; customers that boast about your product or service, and that it bring friends with them.

—W. Edwards Deming

Remember, if your students are happy, their parents will most likely be happy. This doesn't mean to give them everything they want; it does mean that you should treat them with respect. Great businesses do everything possible to make their customers feel special. Make an effort to keep your students and parents happy. For example, Nordstrom has a history of providing quality customer service; its motto is to provide quality items and quality service. This doesn't mean that the customers get everything they want. It does mean that customers will be treated like royalty. Nordstrom customers will sometimes pay more for items because of how they are treated. Treat each parent and student like your number one customer. Go above and beyond providing quality customer service. You want them to feel great about your services and continue sending their children to you.

Promote Patriotism

There can be no fifty-fifty Americanism in this country. There is room here for only hundred-percent Americanism.

—Theodore Roosevelt

Make patriotism important in your school. Grandparents, parents, and community members love schools that promote patriotism. Write letters to those in the service. Celebrate Memorial Day and Veteran's Day. Invite those in the armed services and the veterans in your students' families and community to school during these celebrations. Don't limit promoting patriotism in schools to only special occasions. Create an environment that promotes patriotism year-round in the school and classrooms. Consider having students announce the Pledge of Allegiance as a part of daily announcements and at the start of convocations. Play the "Star Spangled Banner" before every athletic contest and academic event. Decorate the halls, walls, offices, classrooms, and outside of the school with a patriotic theme. Display flags, banners, posters, and student works that promote our country and values. A patriotic environment helps parents, families, and community members have more positive feelings toward a school. It creates a sense of safety and pride.

Keep the Building Clean and Tidy

Change your thoughts and you change the world.

—Norman Vincent Peale

The broken window theory proposes that a car will not be vandalized until some part of it becomes damaged or in disrepair. For example, Former New York Police Commissioner Bill Bratton left a car for several days in a high crime area of New York City. The car was never touched until a single window was purposely broken. In a matter of days, the car was stripped. Make sure the entire building, including its grounds, lockers and bathrooms, are free of graffiti, broken parts, and disrepair. If something breaks, or someone writes on a wall, it is paramount to fix it as soon as possible. Otherwise, more damage can and will occur in the building.

Keep the buildings looking clean and tidy. Fix anything broken immediately. Remove graffiti in bathrooms, on walls, in lockers, and in the building and grounds immediately. Chipped paint should be patched quickly before people start picking at the spot and making it bigger. Leaders should not wait until little repair problems become bigger repair problems. Pull weeds, trim bushes, prune trees, and remove dead growth from the grounds. Keep the building and grounds free of trash. A well-tended school can change the context of the building into a safe and caring school community. Students, parents, school employees, and the community have more positive feelings toward schools that look nice and are kept in repair. A well-kept building creates a sense of safety. It can change the attitude of students and staff and how they act. A school that needs repair increases negative student feelings and behaviors, whereas well-kept school increases positive student feelings and behaviors.

Make Home Visits

In the middle of difficulty lies opportunity.

—Albert Einstein

Principals should visit the homes of their students. A different perspective can be gained from visiting with the parents in a student's home. It can be an eye-opener for many leaders. Get in the habit of visiting sick students and taking students home when transportation is a problem. Visiting a home can help when trying to find out why a student has been absent from school. It's not uncommon to have families without telephones or whose numbers have changed. Families move. New people will move in and out of the homes. For many of our students, school is the safest place. A student exhibiting inappropriate behavior is a concern, but your perspective can change when you visit a home that has no electricity, no food, filth, absent parents, or people struggling to make ends meet. You gain a whole new perspective when visiting a home.

Use good judgment when making home visits. Consider the neighborhood, environment, community, and families in your school. Make visits with another school employee to ensure safety or use a school police liaison or attendance officer. We don't ask school employees to put themselves in any kind of dangerous predicament. If a negative situation could occur, reconsider making the home visit. Don't judge or condemn parents for their lifestyle and environment. We don't want parents to be defensive and further wedge a negative feeling toward the school. Present yourself in a positive, caring manner.

Have Family Night Activities

Call it a clan, call it a network, call it a tribe, call it a family. Whatever you call it, whoever you are, you need one.

—Jane Howard

Friends are treasures.

—Horace Burns

Develop family night activities in your school. Have a back-to-school night. Incorporate chili suppers, fish fries, reading, movie, recreation, and carnival nights, as well as pep rallies. Develop parent education nights to teach parenting skills. Use all of these nights to establish communication between the school and parents. Start adult education nights to teach computer and other educational courses. Parents and community members will appreciate the good will from the school and principal. These nights are a good opportunity to develop and enhance positive relationships with all school groups.

Get Involved
in Your School District

United we stand, divided we fall.

—Aesop

If you are a high school principal, plan activities with the middle and elementary schools. Be creative. High school students enjoy collaborative programs with middle and elementary school students. Likewise, the younger students will enjoy spending time with older students. You want to create an environment where the students get to visit their respective schools. People have a more positive attitude toward schools that they have personally visited and been active with. Special elementary or middle school nights at ball games are also good ideas.

Use the high school for elementary or middle school events. For example, one high school had a negative public perception. It was a wonderful school, but many students and parents had no idea how wonderful the school was. The elementary and high school principals decided to take the elementary students of the month to the high school to eat lunch with the principals. Both principals would take the students on a tour and highlight the wonderful things going on in the school. The students had a different perception of the school once they visited it. They shared their experiences with other students and parents. The students couldn't wait to get to this high school. Even parents started commenting how wonderful the high school was and couldn't wait for their children to attend it. This small program helped change the perception of this particular high school.

Display Student Work in the Community

We all have possibilities we don't know about. We can do things we don't even dream we can do.

—Dale Carnegie

Without a sense of caring, there can be no sense of community

—Anthony J. D'Angelo

Encourage the community and local businesses to display student work. For example, one local restaurant used laminated pieces of student artwork, poems, and writing samples as place mats. A business could display work on the wall, counters, or on tables. Cover names if student confidentiality is a concern. You get the opportunity to show off all of the great things happening in the school. The student's self esteem will be raised by knowing their work is displayed. Parents will be eager to visit the business showing student work. It's a win-win situation for all.

Publicize Your School Name and Mascot

Build for your team a feeling of oneness, of dependence on one another and of strength to be derived by unity.

—Vince Lombardi

The nice thing about teamwork is that you always have others on your side.

—Margaret Carty

Make your school community a walking billboard that promotes your school name and mascot. A school leader wants to have the school name on everything and anything. Pencils and pens with the school name are better than generic pencils and pens. Soft drink huggies, T-shirts, hats, key chains, posters, notebooks, folders, stickers, and bumper stickers with the school name are all examples of ways to promote your school. Give these items as student and staff rewards, and not only will you be rewarding positive behaviors but also showing the community your school name or mascot.

Help Parents
Help Their Children

To maintain a joyful family requires much from both the parents and the children. Each member of the family has to become, in a special way, the servant of the others.

—Pope John Paul II

Many parents need our help to help their children. It can become frustrating for a teacher to help with a subject, so one can only imagine what many of our parents feel when they attempt to help their children. Take this into consideration and develop parent nights that focus on ways for parents to help their kids. What we assume to be a given might not be a given to our parents. Discuss quiet time when studying, checking plan books for assignments, cleaning out backpacks, nightly reading, technology needs, tutoring, career education, preparing for post–high school education, or who to call when students have questions. Many parents are afraid to ask for fear of appearing inferior or stupid. Share with parents that you don't always understand the assignments and sometimes struggle with helping students with their work. It shows your human side. Parents will think, "If the principal struggles sometimes, then it's OK for me to ask questions on how to help my child." The schools need to create an environment that encourages parents' involvement in their children's education.

Unannounced Visitors

No matter how busy you are, you must take time to make the other person feel important.

—Mary Kay Ash

Nobody gets in to see the wizard, not nobody, not no how!

—Wizard of Oz

Take time to meet with unannounced visitors if possible. Most people understand that you are busy and will appreciate it when you take the time to meet with them. It doesn't have to be lengthy visit, it just needs to be enough time to get the basics of their concerns. If meeting with visitors is not possible, let the person know you will get back to them as soon as possible. Give them a date and time when you will call. Visitors will tell others of how you dropped everything for their visit.

Treat Your Secretary Well

Always be nice to secretaries. They are the real gatekeepers in the world.

—Anthony J. D'Angelo

If a teacher is gone, we call a sub. If a principal is gone, we don't bother. But if the secretary is gone, we might as well close the school.

—Todd Whitaker

Possibly the most important person in your building is your personal secretary. The secretary is the first and last person visitors see when they enter and exit your office. The secretary is the person who represents you on the telephone. Great secretaries can save you several hours of time by restricting unsolicited phone calls, visitors, and redirecting those phone messages to the appropriate personnel. The secretary is the person who is privy to your most confidential issues. If you can't trust your secretary, you should consider a replacement. It's that important. You must have a trusting relationship, a trusting partnership with your secretary. An outstanding secretary is a treasure. If you are fortunate to find one, then cherish this secretary. The secretary's motto should be, "Not on my watch." That means that the secretary will ensure that you are never late with any reports, meetings, or deadlines. The secretary will make sure that you are not surprised.

A great secretary is more than someone who can type and collate papers. The secretary must be able to multitask. Great secretaries have the role of office manager, as well. This is someone who can direct others to the appropriate people; make parents, students, and teachers feel safe, secure, and comfortable; protect your time; ensure the school meets all deadlines; and know whom to call if the school needs something. Treat your secretary well! Make sure that you remember the secretary's birthday, as well as Secretary's Day and holidays. A great secretary can make your life so much easier, whereas a poor secretary can make your life miserable.

Make Every School Employee Feel Like Part of Your School Family

Treat your family like friends and your friends like family.

—Anonymous

Leaders need to remember that a school has numerous employees in addition to teachers. A school may have secretaries, custodians, bus drivers, nurses, assistants, day care employees, cafeteria employees, therapists, speech therapists, specialists, and itinerant staff, depending on the school. Some employees will be part-time. Many employees will come into your building only a few times a week. Schools have daytime and evening staff. It is common for these employees to feel as though they are not part of the staff. A principal needs to think of ways to make all employees feel that they are part of the school team. Remember to celebrate special days or weeks that highlight their professions. For example, the principal could bring treats for cafeteria worker's day, nurse's week, custodian's day, and bus driver's day.

Have special treat weeks for groups who do not have a recognized day. Encourage these employees to be active in leadership roles. For example, one school had the day assistants in charge of fund raising and their day-care workers in charge of safety patrol guards. They took an active leadership role and were involved with the teachers in the building.

Be sure to include part-time staff in the decision-making process. You should look for a special room or corner that part-time employees can call their own when working at your school. Make them feel that your school is their school. Be sure to introduce them to your faculty members. Include their names on your school directory, give them name badges and school shirts, and invite them to faculty luncheons and get-togethers. Ask their opinions. Finally, ensure that every employee receives your newsletters, e-mails, and memos. Special treatment and hospitality will not go unnoticed and helps to increase the climate and culture of your school.

Support Substitute Teachers

No one can make you feel inferior without your consent.

—Eleanor Roosevelt

When people say they work at a good school, what do they mean?

—C. D. Glickman

Any guests in the building are to be treated with respect. One person could share his or her experiences with over a hundred different people. A principal wants the perception of the school to be positive. A bad experience could result in a substitute teacher refusing to sub again in your building. This message will be conveyed to others that your school is a place where you don't want to go, much less send your kids.

The principal needs to support all substitutes. Many students feel that it's OK to be rude and discourteous to substitute teachers. Even some parents feel that it's acceptable to torment substitutes, as they will share through stories of their youth. This sends a message that it's OK to treat substitutes with less respect than the regular teachers. Rude and unacceptable behavior should not be tolerated. Instill a philosophy that all employees, including substitute teachers, are to be treated with proper respect. One grade-level team made a rule that any student name left by the substitute teacher would receive a consequence on the regular teacher's return. This rule was posted in the room. The rule was discussed with students several times during the school year. Students were always reminded that the consequence would occur if their names were left when the teacher was absent. When the teacher returned, there would be consequences (with rare exceptions).

Support Mistakes
and Risk Taking

Behold the turtle. He makes progress only when he sticks his neck out.

—James B. Conant

Principals need to encourage staff to be creative and innovative, and to take risks by supporting employee efforts. Let staff members know that you appreciate their efforts if failure occurs. Don't criticize mistakes; you want staff to feel comfortable trying new ideas. Some teachers have learned the hard way not to take risks and will teach the same way their entire career. Not all students learn in the same way. Creativity and innovation is all the more important if schools are to adapt teaching methods to the wide range of learning styles. Mistakes must be supported if teachers are going to take risks; they are part of the learning process. Schools need teacher creativity and teachers who think out of the box. The fastest and surest way to shut down all innovation is to nit-pick or lecture teachers when they make mistakes. Teachers will stop trying because the risk of making a mistake is too painfully high. In contrast, if a principal wants a building full of teachers creating and discovering new ways to teach kids, they will have to support mistakes and encourage teachers' efforts when they stumble.

Cash (1997) reported that effective leaders rewarded innovation, honored creativity, and tolerated failure. Develop a motto: "If it doesn't work, we'll evaluate, adjust, and try again." A trusting relationship must exist between the employees and principal. If trust is high, employees will be more willing to try new ideas. If trust is low, employees will not be as willing to try new ideas. Very few are willing to take risks if the leader criticizes failures. It is safer to keep doing things the same way than to take risks that might fail. A leader needs to remember to support all employees when taking risks. Research indicated that significant differences existed between how principals supported risk taking of their effective teachers and their ineffective teachers (Fleck, 2003). Teachers who struggle are the very ones who need the most support from the principal if they are to try something different. Otherwise, they will continue to do what they have always done. Doing things the same way will produce the same ineffective results. The principal needs to support ideas that are research based and well planned by teachers. The principal's role thereafter is to give support and monitor their progress.

Admit Mistakes

You know, by the time you reach my age, you've made plenty of mistakes, and if you've lived your life properly, so you learn. You put things in perspective. You pull your energies together. You change. You go forward.

—Ronald Reagan

Be not ashamed of mistakes and thus make them crimes.

—Confucius

If a mistake has been made, address it and move on. Don't try to cover up a mistake. The truth will usually surface. Any mistake not admitted will cause others not to trust you and your decisions. Trust is important. People see through attempts to mask a mistake. What we do in education is too important not to be trusted. Many are looking for a confrontation, and admitting a mistake eliminates the argument. It's hard to argue when you say, "I was wrong. We blew it. We won't let that happen again. Sorry it happened; we will make things right." People will respect you if you admit mistakes and make sincere efforts to correct them. It also develops trust when you don't cover up mistakes. Trust levels will increase if a leader is honest. If a future situation occurs, the community members will be more tolerant of failure because of your philosophy of admitting mistakes and quickly working toward correction. President John F. Kennedy accepted responsibility during the Bay of Pigs. President Kennedy said, "I messed up. Next question?" There was very little to say, and it built a high level of trust with the country. Don't hide mistakes. Don't make excuses. Don't blame others. Take responsibility and admit mistakes. Leaders are not expected to be perfect, only human.

Don't Gossip
or Listen to Gossip

He who permits himself to tell a lie once, finds it much easier to do it a second and third time.

—Thomas Jefferson

What kills a skunk is the publicity it gives itself.

—Abraham Lincoln

People who spread gossip, lies, and negativity are like a cancer. You must stop a cancer before it spreads to the rest of the organization infecting the entire school system. Let others know the facts, and let your actions speak for you. People will soon learn that the gossiper is trouble and will distance themselves. You need to be a role model and resist the temptation to engage in telling tales and gossiping. A leader who gossips or spreads gossips forfeits their right to lead.

Keep Friends Close and Enemies Even Closer

Forgive enemies, but never forget their names.

—John F. Kennedy

Remember your friends in the school community. Seek their advice. Listen to their thoughts. Friends will give you wise council, whereas enemies may seek to sabotage your efforts. Keeping enemies close may help you gain their confidence with the hope that they would be neutral on school plans. They might not be in favor of your decision, but they might not sabotage decisions if you work diligently to gain their confidence. Neutral enemies will allow you to concentrate your efforts on persuading others to accept your school decisions and plans. Also, a close enemy may let intentions slip. It's better to keep enemies close and know their intentions rather than at a distance and have to guess their thoughts.

Consider a classroom, which is typically divided up in three parts. One part of the class has exceptional students who cause no problems, are team players, and work hard without direction from the teacher. These students are a small percentage of the class and can be counted on to do what is right. Another part of the class is made up of students who are defiant, rebellious, and cause problems in the class. These students make up a small percentage in the class and will most likely ignore authority requests. The largest part of the class is the indecisive group. These students are in the middle. They can be persuaded to do what is right as easily as to make poor choices. The teacher should try to keep the indecisive group away from the rebel group. Put your efforts into moving the middle group toward the positive group. When you apply this to teachers, you should be pushing more middle-of-the-road people toward the top group while keeping a close eye on the rebel group. If a principal's thoughts focus more on the top group, it will help to neutralize the rebel group's efforts.

Loyalty Is a Two-Way Street

Masters who sacrifice for servants will receive the gift of loyalty.

—Traditional Proverb

The best things in life are never rationed. Friendship, loyalty, love do not require coupons.

—George T. Hewitt

One must show loyalty to get loyalty in return. Principals have to give loyalty to teachers, staff, students, parents, superintendents, and school board members if they hope to have loyalty in return. Loyalty can help a principal when a tough decision has to be made. Employees are more likely to help the principal with the community stakeholders if the principal has developed a positive relationship and shown employee loyalty.

What is your first reaction when a parent or superintendent complains about a teacher? Do you believe the accusation, or do you respond that it doesn't sound like the teacher but offer to check it out? Do you immediately think that the complaint is plausible, or do you defend the teacher but promise to investigate the matter? Do you accuse the teacher, or do you try to gather information to further your understanding? Loyalty works both ways. If you want teachers to defend you, then you must be willing to fight for them as well. This doesn't mean that you should defend a person who is wrong, but it does mean defending a person until evidence proves otherwise. Loyalty is a two-way street in that principals will defend the actions of employees, superintendents, and school board members, and the same groups will defend the actions of the principal. Principals need to show loyalty to their employees if they hope to have loyalty in return. When parents complain to central office administrators, the principal needs to support the staff. This sign of loyalty will be returned when the principal has to make a tough decision. For example, if the principal has to make a decision that is not popular, teachers will show their loyalty by calming the parents and students. The alternative is that teachers will do very little to help in a difficult situation if loyalty is not present between the principal and staff. A lack of loyalty makes it easy for staff to add fuel to a fire or do nothing to help you during a stressful situation.

Don't Bad-Mouth Your Leaders

Example is not the main thing in life—it is the only thing.

—Albert Schweitzer

A principal cannot bad-mouth the school district's leadership. It is important for school employees to be positive. Bad-mouthing the school district's leadership is wrong for several reasons. First, bad-mouthing school board members and central office administrators is not fair to them. They do not have an opportunity to set the record straight when you bad-mouth them behind their backs. What if the statements are incorrect or are taken out of context? The old adage that there are many sides to every story is correct. How many times have parents called with a complaint with only their children's side of the story? Second, it is not ethical. We accepted a position that was based on us working for them. Third, it is not right. We hope that our school board and central office will show loyalty to us. We should give the same loyalty and show the same respect toward them. Fourth, negativity in the classroom, school, and school community helps no one. Why encourage an environment of negativity? Why put your employees in a bad mood? It's not good for them, the students, or you. Putting your staff in a bad mood will increase the number of students being sent to the office and the number of employee sick days used. It will also increase the number of staff complaints and create an overall bad mood. Putting your staff in a bad mood will decrease student learning. The leader needs to create an environment that is positive. Look for positives, not negatives.

Be Tactful
When Correcting Your Boss

Advice is like snow; the softer it falls, the longer it dwells upon, and the deeper it sinks into the mind.

—Samuel Taylor Coleridge

There is nothing more frightful than ignorance in action.

—Johann Von Goethe

If you feel that your superiors made a gross mistake, then let them know. Look for an opportunity to privately let them know they may be making an error. Telling them in private lets them save face. No one wants to be shown their errors in public. Some ways to voice your concerns include: "Did you consider. . . ?" "I know you know that. . . ." "I don't have to tell you but. . . ," A good superior will remember your professionalism and actions.

Learn to Handle Complaints to Your Superiors

To hear complaints is wearisome to the wretched and the happy alike.

—Samuel Johnson

Principals will occasionally have central office personnel and school board members who only call with bad news. Keep this in mind when they call you. Consider their years of experience or if they have principal experience when they call with parent or community complaints. How many years of experience do they have as a principal? Do they have experience as the dean of discipline? How many years has it been since they served as a principal? Is this a political decision?

Educators and school board members tend to be a nurturing lot and will give subtle messages to parents that complaints will be addressed to their pleasure. Many school board members and central office administrators are politicians. Parents tend to get the idea that central office personnel and school board members will reverse principal decisions. Also, the larger the school system, the more central office personnel will be available until parents reach an accommodating ear. It's like a pinball machine. The ball bounces around until it hits something that dings and gives off points. Principals will receive calls from central office and school board members who like to give suggestions. Most central office and school board members mean well, but some can cause headaches. Some central office personnel will want to offer advice on how they would handle the situation or persuade you to give in on your decision. Principals cringe when they hear the words, "Is this the hill you want to die on?" Resist the temptation to ask, "Is there any hill you're willing to die on? Because I haven't seen any hill you have been willing to die on." If you find yourself with too many telephones calls, schedule a time to let central office administrators and school board members know how you address parent concerns. Explain every painstaking step of how you address parent concerns. Also, explain that if this behavior continues, then they should glue telephones to their ears because parents will learn to jump over you and go straight to any person who gives them an ear. Principals should tell central office personnel and school board members that they hired a principal to address school building concerns so they wouldn't have to do two jobs.

Learn to Handle
School Board Requests

Be sure you put your feet in the right place, then stand firm.

—Abraham Lincoln

Occasionally, a principal will get a request to do a task or grant a favor. A principal has to be conscious of school board members who attempt to micromanage, intimidate, or rob their time with requests. A principal has to stop these behaviors when they become habitual. Favorite techniques to deter these requests are: First, e-mail every board member and your superior explaining that you will look into their request and get back to them immediately. State the request in the e-mail so everyone can see the request. Follow this up by sending answers to everyone at the same level and above.

For example, if a school board member makes a reasonable request, let the person know that you will grant the request; but also send your response to the rest of the school board, as well as all of your superiors. Everyone receives the answer to the same request. You want to eliminate board members who are trying to play the game of one-upmanship. This technique also helps for the rest of the school board members and your superiors to quietly address this breach of etiquette. A second technique to use is to ask the school board member, "Do you mind putting it in writing?" People hate to put requests in writing. Be careful when you use this technique. You have to consider the request. Use this technique when you feel uncomfortable with attempts to micromanage or intimidate you into a decision.

3

Ending
the School Year

Let Staff Know
that the Evaluation Will Include
Both Commendations
and Recommendations

The way I see it, if you want the rainbow, you gotta put up with the rain.

—Dolly Parton

Evaluations don't have to be a stressful experience. Let staff know that each evaluation will focus on both commendations and recommendations. Every person has strengths that can be accentuated. Likewise, every employee can improve and should seek ways to do so. A continuous school improvement plan should include a continuous staff improvement plan. Improvement is a continuous journey, not a destination.

Students, schools, and society are continuously changing. Nothing stays the same. Staff should be expected to change with the changing times. Teachers and their methods will have to change to meet the demands of the future. This is a vital reason to let staff know that everyone will have staff improvement recommendations. It might mean that the very best teacher in the school, district, and state receives a recommendation that states, "Continue to seek and take advantage of professional development and learning opportunities." This is not a criticism but a recommendation to take advantage of professional development opportunities. A leader needs to calm the fears that come with an evaluation. Trust is the key. The principal and employee must have a trusting relationship. Employees must feel comfortable that principal recommendations will help them grow as a professionals.

Finally, encourage employees to set goals each year and use them in the evaluation process. The principal and teacher might write professional development improvement goals together. Developing teacher improvement goals together will help nurture and build a trusting relationship.

Have a Good Relationship with the Unions and Associations

It is understanding that gives us an ability to have peace. When we understand the other fellow's viewpoint, and he understands ours, then we can sit down and work out differences.

—Harry S. Truman

Many leaders feel that an adversarial relationship exists between the unions and associations and the administrators. A principal should keep in mind that unions and associations represent people who have families, pay taxes, want to do a good job, live in the community, and are people just like us. The relationship between a leader and the members of the unions and associations can be strained at times, especially during contract talks, but it can be amenable. One way to keep a positive relationship is to call union and association representatives if you have question concerning the contract. Let them know what you are considering and ask their opinions as it relates to the contract. Ask the representatives, "What is your interpretation of the contract if we do such and such?" They will appreciate how you seek their input before taking action. It may also help to keep you from violating the contract.

Open communication will help develop a positive working relationship with the unions and associations. It will also give the union and association representatives a heads-up in the event one of their members calls with a question pertaining to your plan. Sometimes a principal will need to have a discussion with an employee concerning expectations or their actions. This can be stressful, especially if an employee brings a representative with them when you address concerns. Unions and associations want employees to give an honest day's work for an honest day's pay. The union and association representatives want employees to do well, follow policies and rules, and serve as positive role models. They do not want members who abuse their rights. Union and association representations want principals to be fair and give due process. A principal needs to be open, factual, and fair. Explain your expectations and develop a plan for employee success. The best advice is to treat someone as you would want to be treated: fairly, with dignity and respect. Unions and associations have no problems if you are fair. Communication will help build trust and make your leadership plans go smoother.

Become Results Oriented

Any activity becomes creative when the doer cares about doing it right, or doing it better.

—John Updike

Some people wait so long for their ship to come in, their pier collapses.

—John Goddard

Using data is the key to becoming results oriented. How can anyone know where they are going without knowing where they have been? How do leaders know if they are doing the right things without some sort of data collection? How do principals know potential areas of growth without studying data? Data are essential if schools are to work on increasing student achievement and staff improvement, as well as planning professional development. A leader needs to encourage all staff members to study school data consistently.

Data and being held accountable tend to make principals and teachers feel uneasy. Schmoker (1996) claims that educators avoid data because of fear: the fear to reveal strengths and weaknesses. He further discusses that using data will stimulate schools to work on action and planning improvement strategies instead of ignoring data and promoting inaction and inefficiently. Remember that there is more to data than state testing results.

Encourage teachers to gather their own data. Use teacher results. Conduct surveys. Use assessments. Use portfolios. A principal needs to have frequent conversations using data to plan improvement. Use the data to plan a course of action. It is important to remember to discuss data, action, and improvement with every staff member. Research conducted found principals were more concerned with results than methods of their more effective teachers than those of their ineffective teachers (Fleck, 2003).

Finally, resist the temptation to make excuses for not being results oriented. Many principals and teachers state that improvement is challenging for a number of reasons: too many special needs, impoverished, and at-risk students; too little money for professional development; uncaring and unhelpful parents; and the expectation to do more as funds decrease. Although all this might be true, we cannot let these concerns prevent us from ignoring data and working toward school and student improvement. Remember to start from where you are and use the data to become results oriented toward continuous improvement.

Don't Accept Status Quo

The sad truth is that excellence makes people nervous.

—Shana Alexander

The man who has accomplished all that he thinks he has worthwhile has begun to die.

—E. T. Trigg

Instill pride in your staff to keep improving. Don't accept the status quo. Set expectations and don't settle for anything less. Become a general who instills the message, "We're not holding anything." A large part of leading is to be determined to set and reach goals, always adjusting to reach higher goals.

Jack Welch, former General Electric CEO, encouraged his staff to set "stretch" goals. Stretch goals would seem to be just at the edge but still attainable. Once attained, new goals would be set and stretched toward a new sight. Keep stretching your goals and keep moving forward. For example, set goals for a percentage of students passing all or portions of state testing at the brink of what you feel is attainable. On the one hand, goals must not be too high, because you don't want staff to give up before you begin. On the other hand, don't make your goals too easy. Find a good balance that moves staff out of their comfort zone but leaves staff members with the willingness to roll up their sleeves and advance toward the goals. Once reached, move expectations a little further toward a new goal destination.

Don't Hold Grudges

An eye for an eye makes the whole world blind.

—Mahatma Gandhi

Kindness can become its own motive. We are made kind by being kind.

—Eric Hoffer

I am an optimist. It does not seem too much use being anything else.

—Winston Churchill

Leaders cannot hold grudges. You must eliminate all negative thoughts toward people who upset you. Clear your mind every day. Look forward to the new day as a day to help others in spite of their attitudes and shortcomings. Holding grudges will affect your future decisions, attitude, personal life, and health. Learn to forget past offenses; think ahead to a new day, a new beginning.

Monitor Spending

Beware of little spending, a small leak will sink a ship.

—Benjamin Franklin

Money talks. . . but all mine ever says is good-bye.

—Anonymous

Principals have to monitor spending in their building. Make it a priority to stay under budget. Too many people in education spend money that they would not spend if it were their own personal money. If a staff member wants to buy an item, ask a few simple questions. How will it be used? How does it apply to the academic standards? What other activities will be used with the purchased item? What could you do differently that would cost less? Could you write a grant to get the desired item? Could you get it donated?

Encourage staff members to submit a "wants and needs" list each year. A *want* item is something that is desired, whereas a *needs* item is a must item for school.

Make Safety a Priority

The buck stops here.

—Harry S. Truman

Keep your building safe. Encourage staff to immediately report safety concerns to the office. Complete work orders, date them, and let the appropriate person know about the problem. Make sure to restrict use of the area until the safety concern is corrected. A principal needs to walk the building on a regular basis looking for potential problems. Talk to staff in their respective areas. Engage in regular conversations with the custodian about repairs. Motivate the custodian to take ownership in making the school safe. Some repairs are beyond custodial responsibility and may require the help of others to correct.

If these repairs are ignored or do not happen in a timely manner, or if money is not allocated for repairs, then submit your safety concerns in writing. Stating safety concerns on a repair order tends to get superiors, custodians, or maintenance employees moving faster to address them. For example, the work order could state, "Ceiling lights and brackets in the gymnasium are loose. They need to be reattached to the brackets hanging from the ceiling. Please make this a top priority. Safety is a concern, because the lights and brackets could fall and possibly injure students or personnel." Be sure to keep a dated office copy. Additional dated copies should follow in a timely manner. Don't assume that completing one work order releases you from any obligation. Keep sending copies to show your concern. Lawsuits are too common. It's better to pay a little more now than a lot more later because of a lawsuit. The National Association of Secondary School Principals has an outstanding Safety and Security Checklist that is highly recommended. It is a quick checklist for all areas in a school for safety concerns.

Delegate Responsibility and Authority

Motivation is everything. You can do the work of two people, but you can't be two people. Instead, you have to inspire the next guy down the line and get him to inspire his people.

—Lee Iacocca

A principal cannot do it all. Good leaders learn to use their staff. Whitaker (1997) cited one major difference between effective and less effective schools was the identification and use of effective teachers at the more effective schools. Every spring, ask staff members to list committees and activities that they wish to help with for the upcoming year. Your best employees might be in charge of a few more school functions, but make sure that every employee has the opportunity to be the leader of a school activity. Everyone has talents, and most people want to contribute. It's the leader's responsibility to figure out how to use every person in the school. New employees might be placed with a veteran for a year, knowing they will lead that activity the following year. Limit their leadership roles in the early years, because you want them to concentrate on standards, curriculum, and their classrooms.

It's been said that 20% of the employees do 80% of the work. Staff will do this for a while, but they will burn out over the years and stop contributing in activities. If leaders assign employees too many assignments, their contributions will diminish. Leaders learn to make everyone a school leader in an organization. Learn to tell your staff members that they are responsible and have your complete confidence. However, leaders must have an understanding of what each committee, employee, and team leader is doing. Leaders must set visions with their respective groups and then give power to conduct business.

Giving support becomes your task as the process is monitored. Learn to lead by being led. You need to be careful not to give too much guidance, to avoid becoming a crutch. Resist the temptation to micromanage employees. Staff might stumble, but let them work through each learning experience. Everyone has to gain experience, and some may make mistakes. Help staff members to reflect on their performances. Employees will surprise you with great results if given the right amount of confidence and support.

Make Changes if Necessary

Swift justice demands more than just swiftness.

—Potter Stewart

Drastic action may be costly, but it can be less expensive than continuing inaction.

—Richard E. Neustadt

Occasionally, leaders will find themselves working with a person who cannot respond to leadership roles. Being patient is a virtue. Leaders must help the staff by being supportive and sharing a desired vision. Possible suggestions may be helpful if the staff needs further assistance. An organization will work better if all employees have leadership roles. Sometimes leaders may be faced with making personnel changes and possibly removing a staff member from a particular leadership role. A principal has to receive regular progress reports from the staff. If an assigned leader is still incapable of responding with assistance, gradually remove that person from the position. You might assign other tasks that are more in line with their talents. Be sincere with employees, and let them know that you appreciate their efforts. Allowing them to stay with the group but shifting their power to another employee is another possibility. If possible, help them save their dignity when removing them from a leadership role.

Record Mistakes
and Evaluate

The only real mistake is the one from which we learn nothing.

—John Powell

We teach people that mistakes are like skinned knees for little children. They're painful, but they heal quickly, and they're learning experiences. My people are covered with the scars of their mistakes. They've lived out in the field; they've been shot at; they've been hit in every part of their bodies; and they're real. By the time they get to the top, their noses are pretty well broken. The chances of their getting there with a clean nose are zero.

—H. Ross Perot

Great leaders use some sort of a problem-solving model when making major decisions. Most approaches include gathering and analyzing data, considering pros and cons, developing plans, communicating and implementing plans, and evaluating the plans. A step often overlooked is the evaluating phase. A leader needs to record mistakes, receive feedback, and thoroughly analyze the process. What went wrong? What could have been done differently? What will I do next time? It's not easy to dissect your mistakes, but this phase is crucial to learning. Great leaders learn to persevere.

Gather Information

Luck is a matter of preparation meeting opportunity.

—Oprah Winfrey

There are no facts, only interpretations.

—Friedrich Nietzsche

Gathering information is the first step. Learn to gather as much information as possible when making decisions. There is no excuse for not being prepared, especially with today's technology. The Internet has made gathering data faster and easier, but you shouldn't stop with information from technology sources. Desegregate state testing data and talk to peers, mentors, parents, researchers, university employees, businesses, community members, and friends to get information. These talks will always lead to more names to call. It's a continuous and endless supply of informational resources. Ask employees their thoughts. A common practice is to rely on those closest to you for information, but a leader does not want too many individuals who think alike. Create a diverse group when developing a fact-finding committee.

Study the best practices. Cherish approved methods. Go to the library. Read magazines and books. Get the facts. Read as much as possible, and read from as many sources as possible. Others will be impressed with your homework skills. Learn to synthesize the information. Read it. Study it. Reflect and review the information.

Check References

There ought to be so many who are excellent, there are so few.

—Janet Erskine Stuart

Thoroughly check the references of prospective employees. As principal, you should spend an enormous amount of time checking the background, education, experience, and work history of those seeking employment in your building. Look to see if there are any lapses in employment. If so, ask about it. Do the references give glowing recommendations or average recommendations? Average recommendations might have been the best recommendation the applicant could get. Call previous employers and ask questions that pertain to the position you are looking to fill. It is important to call people who were direct supervisors of the applicant. A boss may have more relevant information, as compared with information from a friend, neighbor, coworker, or clergy member, but don't discount the comments of others, especially coworkers. They might be able to share some perspectives on the person's work ethic, dependability, teamwork, leadership, and personality. Consider whether or not the person was honest on the application.

Make a list of questions before you call references. Check your district policies and state laws on what you may ask applicants and references. You could ask the references questions such as the following: Is the applicant dependable? Trustworthy? Responsible? Is the applicant a team player? Is the applicant someone you could count on to lead a project? How long did the applicant work for you? Why did the applicant leave? What were the applicant's responsibilities? Did the applicant report directly to you? If you had an opening would you hire this person again? What are this person's strengths? Weaknesses? Can you think of any reason not to hire this person?

Ask references for names and numbers of people who have worked with the applicant. Call these people. They might give you a different perspective than references identified by the applicant. If you get a funny feeling, make sure to investigate the applicant even further. A principal can never spend too much time making sure to get the right person for the job. It is time well spent. Employers who do a poor job investigating prospective employees will end up paying later. It's better to take more time to ensure that you hire the best person rather than spending more time trying to improve the wrong person hired or, worse, spending even more time trying to discharge a poor employee. Outstanding employees will save principals time because they don't need as much direction. It's easy—spend time now hiring a great employee or spend more time later with a poor employee.

Hire the Best Available

You're only as good as the people you hire.

—Ray Kroc

Hire the best talent available. Don't hire friends, friends of friends, or people who are not the best. First, it can be difficult when a prospective employee has political connections. Resist the temptation to hire someone because of that person's connections. If the superintendent or school board puts pressure on you, submit your recommendation in writing. They can still hire the person they desire, but your recommendation is in writing. People can sometimes acquire convenient amnesia and forget the facts over time. Something in writing will eliminate any future problems such as blaming the principal for hiring the wrong employee.

Another potential mistake is to hire someone who has subbed or worked in a principal's current building. Resist the temptation to hire someone based on loyalty. A common reason people use is, "They have paid their dues." Although it may be true that principals should show employee loyalty, it is more important to show loyalty to the students. What we do in education is too important to hire less than the best. Students, parents, and the community members deserve the best school employees—not employees based on political connections and loyalty. Create a value system where you hire employees based on achievement, experience, and talents.

Make Job Applicants Feel Special

It's only eighteen inches between a pat on the back and a kick in the pants.

—Unknown

Make those who apply for a job feel special. People will understand if they don't get a position. It doesn't take any more effort from the principal to make others feel special and help their self-esteem. It's common for applicants to share the interview experience with family, friends, and acquaintances. They will always share positive comments made by the principal. If possible, share positive comments specific to their interview or qualifications. "Your portfolio is excellent. I talked to your references and they gave you glowing recommendations. I talked to your present employer and they would hate to lose you but understand why you're considering this position. I like how you handle yourself when presented with questions."

Another consideration is how to handle those who presently volunteer or work in your building. For example, consider a teacher from your building who applies for an assistant principal's position. If the teacher does not get the position, you should personally let the person know that. If she is good, let her know that there was strong competition and it was tough to choose. Furthermore, let her know that you appreciate her efforts. Tell her not to get discouraged because this one didn't work out. Encourage her to keep trying because she is a good and talented teacher. You could say, "It was a strong talent pool. It was tough, but I thought that this other person was what we needed right now. Don't get discouraged; it will eventually happen."

However, if the teacher is not an excellent candidate, you can let him know that you appreciate his efforts, taking the time to prepare for this interview, and desiring to be more active in leadership. In both cases, look for ways to keep all the applicants active and remaining positive in your building. You don't want staff to quit trying and become disgruntled. When an employee does not get a position, the principal should use this opportunity to help her get more involved in your building. Let her know that it will prepare her for that next opening. Let her know that you need her and appreciate her efforts. Help her get more active in leadership roles.

Don't Be Insecure

I not only use all the brains I have, but all I can borrow.

—Woodrow Wilson

Great leaders learn to hire the best, hopefully, hiring people brighter than themselves. Unfortunately, many leaders will hire inferior employees to make sure they look better or have the school community dependent on them. Principals should not feel threatened by an employee or a peer. Principals should have the philosophy, "I have a building full of people who make me look good." Leaders should use the best people in the school for each assignment. Don't become insecure that a person will look brighter than you. Some insecure persons will limit placing staff in leadership roles because they are afraid that the staff member could be promoted over them someday or outshine them. Recommend talented individuals to serve on school, district, and state committees. Also, learn to ask questions. An inferior person may not ask questions with the notion that they will look foolish. It's better to ask questions and understand than to not ask questions and not know. Leaders need to get over being insecure and do what's best for the school.

Study the Experts

What ever you are . . . Be a good one.

—Abraham Lincoln

Get in the habit of reading and studying great leaders. Look at leaders in all areas and fields. Study past and present leaders. Study their actions. Expand your reading beyond educational leadership experts. A great leader in one field might be able to shed light for greatness in your area. Study fields in management, sales, human relations, psychology, history, religion, motivation, communication, and leadership. Use their positives in your area. Follow their leadership examples and apply it in schools. Read more than the local paper. Consider subscribing to a national newspaper like the *New York Times* or the *Washington Post*. Also, all ages, all persons in your building, district, and community have talents. Examine, study, and ask questions pertaining to their strengths. They might be able to share secrets that come naturally for them. Several authors have numerous books and articles that are valuable for those in school leadership. Learn from these leaders. Embrace their ideas. Create your own library of experts. Some personal education favorites and suggested authors include the following:

- Roland Barth
- Ken Blanchard
- Peter Deming
- Peter Drucker
- Michael Fullan
- Howard Gardner
- John Gardner
- Alan Glathorn
- Jonathon Kozol
- Robert Marzano
- Elaine McEwan
- Phillip Schlechty
- Thomas Sergiovanni
- Todd Whitaker

Suggested Books

If you think education is expensive, try ignorance.

—Derek Bok

Recommended books for school leaders are shown in the following list. Some authors have numerous books and articles not included on this list. They are included on the *study the experts* list. The following list is in no specific order.

- *The Principal's Handbook* by Pam Robbins and Harvey Alvy
- *Achievement Now!* by Donald Fielder
- *The Power of Reading* by Stephen Krashen
- *First Days of School* by Harry Wong
- *Best Practices* by Zemelman, Daniels, and Hyde
- *Good to Great* by Jim Collins
- *Lincoln on Leadership* by Donald Phillips
- *Monday Morning Leadership* by David Cottrell
- *Zapp* by William C. Byham
- *Understanding by Design* by Grant Wiggins and Jay McTighe
- *Leadership Secrets of Attila the Hun* by Wess Roberts
- *The Tipping Point* by Malcolm Gladwell
- *The Power of Positive Thinking* by Norman Vincent Peale
- *How to Win Friends and Influence People* by Dale Carnegie
- *Results* by Mike Schmoker
- *Seven Habits of Highly Effective People* by Steven Covey
- *Fish* by Lundin, Paul, and Christensen
- *101 Answers for New Teachers and Their Mentors* by Annette Breux
- *Emotional Intelligence* by D. Goleman
- *Understanding and Educating African-American Children* by William Jenkins
- *The Fifth Discipline* by Peter Senge
- *Professional Learning Communities* by Rick Dufour
- *A Framework for Understanding Poverty* by Ruby Payne
- *Etiquette* by Emily Post
- A daily inspirational Bible

Network

Networking is an enrichment program, not an entitlement program.

—Susan RoAne

The time spent identifying your base of contacts is an investment in your success and the success of others with whom you share your resources.

—Susan RoAne

Create a network of friends and business associates. Learn to meet and greet people. Join a club or organization. Become involved in the community. Take an active leadership role in clubs and in the community. Inquire about which community groups are available in your school district. Take an active interest in every person you meet. Learn the names of their families, interests, and dislikes. Take time to remember important details pertaining to each acquaintance. Networking is important to success. Make time each week to contact friends and associates. A quick and brief call will suffice.

Using e-mail or writing letters is another great method to stay in touch with others. This method doesn't make you wait for the person to answer the telephone. People will appreciate that you stay in touch with them. Become active in local, state, and federal education organizations. Consider joining the state and national principals' associations. A person cannot belong and be active with every organization, so pick a few and become active. Reading association news, attending conferences, and networking with other administrators and educators are all beneficial ways to gain knowledge and keep abreast of trends and best practices. The following are a few recommended groups:

- National Association of Secondary School Principals
- National Association of Elementary School Principals
- (State) Association of School Business Officials
- (State) Association of School Principals
- Phi Delta Kappa
- Parent Teacher Organization or Parent Teacher Association
- Association for Supervision and Curriculum Development

Help Others

There is no more noble occupation in the world than to assist another human being—to help someone succeed.

—Alan Loy McGinnis

The power of personal example is the essence of true leadership.

—Steven Covey

Make every effort to help employees, parents, students, and those in the community. Reach out to assist those in need. Use your talents to give guidance, support, and assistance. Spend time weekly helping those who would never be able to pay you back. If career advancement is important, consider that helping others could help your career. A common habit is to only help those ahead of you on a career ladder. Remember that as you climb a career ladder, there will be more people below you. The sheer number of people below you gives you more opportunities to help more people each day. This mathematical possibility of helping more people will increase the possible positive statements about you. Also, each person has family and associates, which increases the number of people feeling good about you. My greatest memories of kindness were from prominent individuals. I knew that they were busy, and I appreciated their acts of kindness. Make it your daily mission to help others who might not be able to advance your career.

Teach Others

Service is the rent we pay for living.

—Unknown

I am only one; but still I am one. I cannot do everything, but still I can do something; I will not refuse to do something I can do.

—Helen Keller

Every leader should spend some time each year teaching others. It doesn't always have to be in a university, at a workshop, or at a conference. It can be a youth-sponsored activity or church activity. It can be at faculty meetings. Organize a parent night activity to teach parents or adults within your community. Organize a time to teach aspiring administrators in both informal and formal settings. Form a group to mentor and counsel. Leaders need some part of their yearly time devoted to teaching others or passing along secrets of success.

Write Grants, Seek Donations

Money is like manure. You have to spread it around or it smells.

—J. Paul Getty

Better to light one candle than to curse the darkness.

—Chinese Proverb

Learn to write grants. It's an easy way to get resources and money for your schools. There is a lot of money each year that is not used. Encourage staff to write grants. If possible, allow staff to attend grant-writing seminars. Consider allowing staff time to write grants during the school day. Hire substitute teachers to teach their classes for part of the day, or bring in guest speakers. Students will enjoy having the principal or a guest with some specific talent for the day while their teacher is given time to work on a grant. Other ideas include paying teachers stipends during the summer or on the weekends.

Instill confidence in your staff that anyone can write a grant. It takes practice and persistence. Grants are an excellent way to bring extra goodies into your school, and writing them helps with employee motivation. Leaders today have to beg for money, equipment, resources, and services more than ever. They cannot be too proud to ask for money, items, donations, and people's time. Incorporate a climate where your entire school community is looking for bargains, discarded items, donations, and stored outdated merchandise. Keep abreast of other schools, churches, universities, and businesses looking to donate materials and equipment. You won't know unless you ask.

Learn Something New
Every Year

The wisest mind has something yet to learn.

—George Santayana

There are no shortcuts to any place worth going.

—Beverly Sills

Leaders need to read, add new skills, and set new professional goals each year. Adding new skills each year should be expected. Society is changing at a rapid pace. Many of our students will have jobs that have not been created yet. Teach others not to be status quo. A principal should set learning goals each year. For example, learn a new language, become a certified trainer in an area, learn new technology skills, take a class, attend a workshop or conference, conduct research, or earn a new degree. Don't become stagnate; learn new skills each year.

Have Written Goals
and Update Them Regularly

I have already achieved all the fame, glory, attention, and adulation any mortal could wish for. Yet I am plagued with the desire for more.

—Unknown

You've got to continue to grow or you're just like last night's cornbread—stale and cold.

—Loretta Lynn

A study showed that 83% of the population does not have goals, and 14% of the population has goals, but not written goals. This 14% group has a plan in mind only. Only 3% of the population has written goals. The study found that the 14% who have goals are 10 times more successful than those who have no goals. The populations who have written goals are three times more successful than the group that has goals that are not written. A person is more likely to achieve a goal if it's written. Many individuals have calendars to mark plans. This is a written goal. Writing it down on the calendar helps to ensure the success of making the appointment. This is a small example of a goal. Successful people learn to write not only short-term goals but also mid- and long-term goals. The principal, staff, and students should have yearly goals that are in writing. Also, leaders should consider showing employees their written goals. First, it will help to give staff members the confidence to write their own goals. Second, it will help motivate the principals to achieve their goals, because they have gone out on a limb and shared them with the staff.

It Is Better
to Do a Few Things Well

A committee is a group that keeps minutes and loses hours.

—Milton Berle

Accomplishing the impossible means only that the boss will add it to your regular duties.

—Doug Lawson

Leaders are expected to serve on committees and to lead tasks. It is better to do a great job on fewer tasks than to try to do too many. Be careful not to spread yourself too thin. A common trap is to try to please superiors or build a powerful resume by participating in too many committees and activities. Each person has 24 hours each day. Each task will limit your effectiveness. It is better to be great on a few tasks than a name on several committees. Encourage each staff member to become a leader on a few tasks, knowing that every person will do a better job this way than serving on too many activities. Also, *burnout* can often occur by attempting to do too much. The leader needs to remember the old adage, "more is less and less is more."

Become
a "Community in Schools Site"

Coming together is a beginning; keeping together is progress; working together is success.

—Henry Ford

Create a "Community in Schools Site Council" within your school. Invite members of the community to your school. Members should include parents, teachers, the principal, the nurse, social workers, and the counselor from the internal school. External school members could include health officials, mental health officials, businesses, social workers, psychologists, therapists, doctors, dentists, community leaders, university leaders, politicians, senior citizens, and nonprofit organizations. Bring these people together in your school to discuss student and family needs. Do an inventory of the strengths and opportunities of your school. Organize monthly meetings with the members of your school community. Discuss the wants and needs of the school, and see which organizations can help meet those needs. Keep notes, and dispense them to all members in a timely manner.

It takes regular discussion and commitment, but it's worth the time. Schools cannot do it all. Student achievement and school improvement can be challenging when students' basic needs are not being met. Create a positive relationship with the community members and get them involved in helping your students and families.

See the School through the Parent's Eyes

Grant that we may not so much seek to be understood as to understand.

—St. Francis of Assisi

Accomplishment will prove to be a journey, not a destination.

—Dwight D. Eisenhower

You need to think about how you would want to be treated if your child went to your own school. What type of school would you want your child to attend? How would you feel? What would you want for your child? What would be your likes and dislikes? How would you like the principal to handle concerns? How would you react to school concerns? How would you like school personnel to treat your child? What type of teacher would you want? What type of school environment would you want? See your school through a parent's eyes and create an environment conducive to what you would want for your own child. Also, consider how you would want to be treated when discussing issues with the principal.

Develop
a Parent Report Card

A Chinese general put it this way: If the world is to be brought to order, my nation must first be changed. If my nation is to be changed, my hometown must be made over. If my hometown is to be reordered, my family must first be set right. If my family is to be regenerated, I myself must first be.

—A. Purnell Bailey

Consider creating a parent report card. The report card should be positive. Don't use it to point out parents who are not involved in their child's school. It could be a checklist with events that parents participate in during the school year. Back-to-school night, open house, fall and spring conferences, honor banquets, parents' night, and family night activities would be a few events that every parent should attend. Encourage parents to attend these events. Have contests for the classrooms with the highest attendance rate. Parents need to take an active participation in their children's education. Be creative in getting parents involved in the school.

Encourage Staff to Attend Professional Development Opportunities

Good timber does not grow with ease. The stronger the wind, the stronger the trees.

—J. Willard Marriott

Encourage your staff to attend professional development opportunities and to stay current on educational issues. This includes encouraging secretaries, nurses, counselors, therapists, aides, and cafeteria staff to stay abreast of the latest educational recommendations in their respective areas. Deming shared that if schools are to achieve effectiveness, job training must be provided for all members of the school, a program of self-improvement must instituted, and there must be a requirement for a continuous learning program (Ubben & Hughes, 1997). All employees need to keep abreast of trends in their respective fields. A staff improvement plan should include pursuing continuing education.

The best always seem to be working to improve their knowledge, their craft. Employees should set two to three goals each year, one of which should focus on professional development. The principal and teachers should discuss goals and have frequent conversations throughout the year asking what did you learn that you did not know? What did you learn that made you revisit old knowledge? Have you been able to practice anything learned? What strategies have you planned to apply your new knowledge? What did you try that didn't go well? What adaptations will you make and try again?

Blase and Blase (1999) reported that teachers consistently rated principals as effective when they encouraged teacher reflection on their professional practices. It seems that principals are more supportive of their most effective staff's efforts in pursuing continuing education opportunities than their less effective staff. Research found that principals differed significantly when encouraging professional development opportunities with more effective teachers than with their ineffective teachers (Fleck, 2003). Awareness of this difference is all the more important for principals to promote an environment that supports all teachers to stay current on educational issues and engage in professional development activities. A possibility is for employees to list all professional development activities attended for the school year. These lists can be used to discuss professional development growth with each employee and plan for the upcoming year.

Consider Staff Strengths
When Assigning Tasks

To build on a person's strengths, that is, to enable him to do what he can do, will make him effective… to try to build on his weaknesses will be… frustrating and stultifying.

—Peter Drucker

A leader needs to consider each person's strengths and weaknesses before assigning tasks. Consider the pros, cons, and opportunities of each task. List each person who could lead or perform that task. Each employee has talents, and leaders should distribute building responsibilities according to employee strengths. No one can do it all and do it well. As the number of responsibilities increases, task effectiveness will decrease. Surround yourself with talented people. Learn to balance assignments and use each employee's strengths so you don't weigh down any one person. Great principals learn to have discussions with staff on their likes, dislikes, preferences, and comfort zone. Principals need to ask, "What do you need from me? Who should I put with you? What can I do to ensure your success on this task? Do you feel comfortable leading this task? How often do you feel we should get together to discuss progress?" The leader wants to put staff in a situation where they may succeed.

Give Each Employee a Budget

I'm living so far beyond my income that we may almost be said to be living apart.

—E. E. Cummings

Few things can help an individual more than to place responsibility on him, and to let him know that you trust him.

—Booker T. Washington

Teach staff members to budget in their areas. For example, consider giving each teacher a certain amount of money to buy school supplies in lieu of buying supplies and administering as needed. It makes employees consider the value of the desired item if they have to pay for it from their own budgets. Employees will use better judgment when they have their own personal budgets instead of a large school budget. It can be too easy to want an item if it comes from the principal's budget instead of their own budgets. Giving budgets can help staff distinguish between needs and wants. Giving budgets can help employees to conserve resources. For example, if employees had to purchase printer cartridges from their own budgets, then it might make them consider how often they use their printers. Budgets allow each teacher to purchase items based on their own specific teaching needs.

Giving budgets sends the message that teachers are professionals and they should know what their individuals needs are for their classrooms. Using the same example, it would allow one teacher to purchase numerous printer cartridges as compared with another teacher who didn't print many items and wanted additional math manipulatives. Also, principals should be training and helping prepare future administrators. Giving budget responsibilities will help employees develop these skills in the event they become administrators or school leaders.

Allow University Students to Work in Classrooms

The price of greatness is responsibility.

—Winston Churchill

Allowing university students to train in teachers' classrooms gets mixed reactions. First, schools have an obligation to help train our future teachers. Classroom experience is invaluable. Who best to give guidance and share in their experiences than outstanding teachers? Experience under the watchful eyes of successful teachers is needed for the next wave of educators. Student-teaching experiences also allow principals to see potential teachers working in their buildings. Many teachers hired by principals gained student-teaching experience in the same building.

However, kids should have the best teacher possible. The best teachers for our kids are the regular classroom teachers. One research study found that the regular teacher and students were not in class together during up to one-third of the school year. One-third! That means during only two-thirds of the year were teacher and students together free of interruptions, field trips, assemblies, speakers, professional development days, and teacher or student absences. Also, it takes an enormous amount of time preparing, mentoring, and training the student teachers.

Here are some suggestions for when you allow university students into classrooms with staff. First, look for teachers with experience. There is no magic number, but consider an excellent teacher with 15 years or more of teaching experience and a master's degree. Consider how many years' experience they have in that specific grade or subject. Second, look at their licenses. Do they have an undergraduate and graduate license in their teaching area? What is their major? Third, allow only your top teachers to have university students who are completing their final student-teaching experience. Each school is different, so your numbers might depend on how many outstanding teachers you have. Fourth, teachers cannot have a student teacher every year. Allow your best teachers to have a student teacher every few years—maybe every other year, but never every year. Try to alternate teachers serving as university mentors, so you will always have a few university senior students in your building. It's exciting to have university students full of wonderment and ideas in a building.

Use Beginning University Students in Your Building

Those who can, teach; those who can't, go into some other much less significant line of work.

—Todd Whitaker

To teach is to learn

—Japanese Proverb

Consider placing beginning university students in teacher's classrooms. University students in their freshman through junior years will gain experience serving in an aide-like role, working with small student groups, and teaching a few sections during this experience. Specifically try to place university students with teachers who have challenging students. Another adult in the room will help as they focus their attention on a few specific students. Also, look for teachers who need to be energized. Consider placing university students in these classrooms. Having a university student full of ideas and eager to get into education can help energize some teachers. Both the university student and the regular teacher gain experiences from each other as they work together.

Finally, don't put university students in mediocre teachers' classrooms. If there is a possibility that it will be a negative experience, don't place the university student in that teacher's room. We want university students to apply positive strategies learned from their classroom experiences. Principals must guard against any university student having a negative experience. We don't want university students to become discouraged because of one negative student teaching experience and leave the teaching profession before they begin. Having a good student-teacher mentor ensures the success rate that university students will have positive student teaching experiences.

Provide Materials and Equipment Needed to Do the Work

If our people are to fight their way up out of bondage, we must arm them with the sword and the shield and the buckler of pride—belief in themselves and their possessions based upon a sure knowledge of achievements in the past.

—Mary Mcleod Bethune

Principals should have teachers complete a "needs and wants" list for the upcoming year. Try to give what you can to ensure teacher success. Consider each teacher's strengths, weaknesses, and teaching style. Each teacher is unique and will have different needs. It can be a waste of money to purchase the same item for every teacher hoping that all the teachers will all use the material. Buy what teachers want, need, and will use with their students. Research shows that principals tend to supply extra resources to their more effective teachers as compared with their less effective teachers (Fleck, 2003). It could be that more effective teachers have shown results and thus are rewarded with more supplies in their classrooms. A second reason could be that principals personally like their more effective teachers better. A leader needs to evaluate needs and wants for all employees. Be careful not to play favorites and look at the needs of the students. Ubben and Hughes (1997) suggested that schools should provide the best available instructional materials. The leader needs to be aware of this tendency and make every effort to support all employees regardless of their ability.

Think About How Decisions Will Affect the Entire School

We cannot tear out a single page of our life, but we can throw the whole book in the fire.

—George Sand

Some decisions are hard. Others are easy, but even easy decisions can sometimes have a detrimental effect on the entire school. A principal must consider what that decision will do for the entire school. A single individual is never more important than the entire organization.

A common mistake is to make decisions based on how an influential person or group would respond to your decision. Another mistake is to make decisions based on a person or group who might complain the loudest. Some administrators do not want battles and will consider this as they ponder their decisions. I've heard some administrators base their entire decision-making philosophy on this question: "Is this the hill I want to die on?"

Yet another mistake is to make a decision based on the philosophy of what's best for an individual person. Your decision could be what's best for one person, but it might also be wrong for the entire school community. It's not easy, but principals need to think through the possible ramifications of each choice. Decisions may have to be based on what is best for the organization and not one individual.

Don't Give Up
Your Power in Writing

Power corrupts, and absolute power corrupts absolutely.

—Lord Acton

Power corrupts, absolute power is kind of neat.

—John Lehman

Aesop's story is a wise one to remember as an administrator. A lion wanted to marry a farmer's daughter. The farmer would not consent to the marriage because he feared the lion's sharp teeth and claws. The lion had his teeth and claws removed, and the farmer promptly beat the lion's brains out. It is better to consider input from parents, staff, teachers, and stakeholders than to create a contract or school board policy based on one group's input. Be careful giving up your strength to the point that a group could "beat your brains out."

I recently watched the popular TV show, *The Apprentice*. Contestants in this reality TV show are given business tasks, and one person is eliminated each week. The leader from the winning team is exempt from elimination the next week. One contestant gave up his exemption status. Perhaps he thought that he gave a stellar performance and would not be fired. Perhaps he thought it would show that he was a team player, or maybe he wanted to show his willingness to go out on a limb with his team. Who knows why he gave up his power? In my opinion, the contestant did give an outstanding performance. He did not deserve to be fired and was probably the strongest during that task. It didn't matter. The contestant had the power of exemption, and he gave up his power. The decision cost him and he was fired.

References

Beck, L. G., & Murphy, J. (1993). *Understanding the principalship: Metaphorical themes, 1920s–1990s*. New York: Teachers College, Columbia University.

Bissel, B. (1992, July). The paradoxical leader. Paper presented at the Missouri Leadership Academy, Columbia, MO.

Blanchard, K., & Bowles, S. (1993). Raving Fans. New York: William Morrow.

Blase, J., & Blase, J. (1999). Principal's instructional leadership and teacher development: Teachers' perspectives. *Educational Administration Quarterly, 35*(3), 349–378.

Bossert, S. (1996). Administrator effects. In Marvin C. Alkin (Ed.), *Encyclopedia of educational research* (pp. 19–22). New York: Macmillan.

Bossert, S., Dwyer, D. C., Rowan, B., & Lee, G. V. (1982). The instructional role of the principal. *Educational Administration Quarterly, 18*(3), 34–64.

Cash, J. (1997). What good leaders do. *Thrust for Educational Leadership 27*, 22–25.

Cottrell, D. (2002). *Monday morning leadership*. Cornerstone, TX: Leadership Institute.

DuFour, R. (1999). Challenging role: Playing the part of principal stretches one's talent, *Journal of Staff Development, 20*(4), 62.

Fleck, F. (2003). *How principals work with their more and less effective teachers*. Unpublished doctoral dissertation, Indiana State University, Terre Haute.

Gates, G., & Siskin, D. (2001). Principal leadership styles and attitudes toward shared decision making with teachers. *Planning and Changing, 32*(3–4), 164–183.

Glatthorn, A. A. (1998). Roles, responsibilities and relationships. In G. R. Firth, & E. F. Pajak (Eds.), *Handbook of research on school supervision* (pp. 374–396). New York: Simon & Schuster.

Johnson, S. M. (1990). *Teachers at work: Achieving success in our schools*. New York: Basic Books.

Krug, S. E. (1992). Instructional Leadership: A constructivist perspective. *Educational Administration Quarterly, 30*(4), 430–443.

Law, S., & Glover, D. (2000). *Educational leadership and learning*. Philadelphia: Open University Press.

Leithwood, K. (1992a). The move toward transformational leadership. *Educational Leadership, 49*(5), 8–12.

Leithwood, K. (1992b). Leadership for school restructuring. *Educational Administration Quarterly, 30*(4), 498–518.

McEwan, E. (1998). *Seven steps to effective leadership*. Thousand Oaks, CA: Corwin Press.

Miller, A. W. (2001). Finding time and support for instructional leadership. *Principal Leadership, 2*(4), 29–33.

National Association of Elementary School Principals. (2001). Leading learning communities: Standards for what principals should know and be able to do. Alexandria, VA: National Association of Elementary School Principals.

National Association of Secondary School Principals. (2002). NASSP statement of values. Reston, VA: National Association of Secondary School Principals.

National Forum on Educational Leadership. (1999). *Effective leaders for today's schools*. Washington, DC: United States Department of Education.

Patterson, J. (2000). *The anguish of leadership*. Arlington, VA: American Association of School Administrators.

Peters, T., & Waterman, R. (1982). In Search of Excellence. New York: Warner Books.

Pierson, R. (2002). *Rita's stories*. Highland, TX: Aha! Process, Inc.

Schlechty, P. (2002). Shaking up the Schoolhouse. San Francisco: Jossey-Bass.

Schmoker, M. (1996). *Results: The key to continuous school improvement*. Alexandria, VA: Association for Supervision and Curriculum Development.

Sergiovanni, T. J. (2001). *The principalship: A reflective practice perspective*. Boston: Allyn and Bacon.

Shoemaker, J., & Fraser, H. W. (1981). What principals can do: Some implications from studies of effective schooling. *Kappan, 63*, 178.

Smith, W., & Andrews, R. (1989). *Instructional leadership: How principals make a difference*. Alexandria, VA: Association for Supervision and Curriculum Development.

Ubben, G. C., & Hughes, L. W. (1997). *The principal: Creative leadership for effective schools*. Needham Heights, MA: Allyn and Bacon.

Whitaker, B. (1997). Instructional leadership and principal visibility. *Clearinghouse, 70*(1), 155–156.

Whitaker, T. (1997). Three differences between "more effective" and "less effective" middle level principals. *Current Issues in Middle Level Education, 6*(2), 54–64.

Whitaker, T., & Valentine, J. (1993). How do you rate? How effective school leaders involve staff members. *Schools in the Middle, 3*(2), 21–24.

Index